FOCUS ON UNDERSTANDING

AND SUPPORT: A Study

in College Management

by

John W. Leslie

Statistical Analysis

by

Charles Newton

Annette L. Bacon

Published by

AMERICAN COLLEGE PUBLIC RELATIONS ASSOCIATION

Washington, D.C. 20036

Contents

List of Tables

List of Charts

Foreword

It seems strange that only 10 or 15 years ago many college presidents refused to give adequate or effective organizational recognition to the fund raising function. Although the raising of funds was vital to the well being of their institutions, many presidents refused to have a "fund raiser" included among their top officers. Somehow it was felt that to call a spade a spade was demeaning or undignified. Hence, the term "development" was born. The development officer in a college or university might have been given responsibility for publicity, public relations, alumni relations, special events and other promotional activities, but it has been clear for years that one of his major responsibilities is to raise money.

In 1957, the American Alumni Council and the American College Public Relations Association jointly undertook the first major study of the development function and obtained a grant from the Ford Foundation to support this endeavor. This study culminated in a conference of college presidents, trustees, development officers and others, which was held at the Greenbrier early in 1958. Among the major results of the study were a more precise definition of what was meant by "development," the dignifying of the fund raising function, and at least the beginnings of a recognition of the importance of the position of the development officer in college management.

In the years following 1958, vice presidents for development rapidly made their appearance along with other vice presidents as principal officers of colleges and universities. The development activity appeared to have been given the organizational recognition needed to carry on the work effectively.

However, it soon became clear that this initial study was but a first step in encouraging the creation of effective development staffs. It was apparent to those who had spent years studying the organization and administration of colleges and universities and to the officers and governing board of the American College Public Relations Association (ACPRA) that there were great disparities in performance and in the effectiveness of development offices. In some cases, the wide range and quality of performance could be explained by factors not easily controlled. These included adverse factors such as the hostility of state legislatures to fund raising by a public institution, and positive elements of strength such as strong tradition of alumni giving. There are, however, other factors affecting performance which are subject to control through good management. These include sound versus unsound organization, a matching of staffing with workload, controls over staff time and effort, cost accounting, evaluation of programs, and a measurement of the results obtained for the time and money expended.

ACPRA is to be commended for not stopping with the solid gains made as a result of the Greenbrier Conference. ACPRA concluded that further efforts were needed to improve development operations and obtained funds from the Esso Education Foundation in 1966 to support a second and, in many ways, far more penetrating study of the development function than had been possible in the 1950s. The purpose of the second study was to get at ways in which to refine and improve the effectiveness of development performance. Yardsticks which could be used to measure the effectiveness were to be identified, tested and applied. The methods of study used and the results of the analyses made are set forth in the chapters which follow.

Here it may be observed that the data obtained from the hundreds of questionnaires distributed and the replies received, from field visits and from personal interviews, provided ample documentation of the fact that there are many opportunities to improve development work. Fortunately, the study also revealed that there are indicators which can be applied to evaluate performance, that certain quantitative measurements can be made, and that the means (primarily electronic equipment) to obtain and analyze quantitative factors are readily available.

The results of this second study are now published. This publication, along with the volume resulting from the 1958 Greenbrier Conference, are landmarks in the growth and improvement of an important aspect of college and university management.

It is highly significant that the ACPRA is not content to rest with the publication of the present volume. ACPRA wisely has made plans for a series of implementation measures to make available the results of the findings from the present study and to provide installation guidelines to those colleges and universities which wish to benefit from the study. At this time when there are great needs and opportunities to improve the management of colleges and universities, it is gratifying to find those who are concerned with one of the principal elements in college and university administration persistently making efforts to improve the functions for which they are responsible. It would be gratifying if others took a leaf from the ACPRA book.

It probably will be desirable to undertake a further review of the development or advancement offices in another five to 10 years. If the implementation of the present study is successful, a follow-up study in the future could be based upon precise data which hitherto have not been available. Good management is not something which is installed in a one-time operation and then lives on forever. Continuing good management results from frequent review of practices, evaluation of performance, and improvement in techniques.

Certainly, no one who looks to the future can question the importance of the need for effective fund raising offices in our colleges and universities, and especially in the private colleges. The population explosion, the pressure of numbers, scientific developments and the proliferation of subject matter, the utilization of new equipment and devices for instructional purposes, the shortage of trained faculty, world tensions, students' attitudes, and inflation all are responsible in varying degrees for the kinds of problems with which individual colleges and universities must deal. Even the well-endowed or "rich" institutions are not immune from the effects of these conditions.

In the October 1967 issue of *Fortune* magazine, there were published data concerning the financial operations of 20 of the country's richest private colleges and universities as measured in terms of endowment per student. If the projections made there are correct, by 1978 the total annual deficit of these colleges will have risen to approximately 17 percent of their projected operating budgets. This imposes a continuing and a substantial fund raising task.

If the situation is this serious with respect to the wealthy colleges, what of those that are less well off? Kingman Brewster, president of Yale University, has stated, "The less well-endowed university is literally finding its back to the wall as it tries to be competitive in faculty, facilities, and programs."

Higher education in America has lived in a continuing state of crisis and the serious or possibly precarious outlook for the future is not to suggest that this crisis cannot be met. To be sure, some colleges may collapse and some may merge with others. However, in well-managed industries, new problems, unforeseen difficulties and new challenges often bring out the best in management. If the past performance and the present interest of the ACPRA are indicative of what we might expect from this organization in the future, it would appear that there will be continuing efforts to strengthen and improve the performance of the development function in our colleges and universities.

Harlow J. Heneman*

* Editor's note: Dr. Heneman was a key participant in the 1958 Greenbrier Conference. Until his recent retirement, he was a general partner in the management consulting firm of Cresap, McCormick and Paget. In that capacity, he directed the firm's educational, health and government division and was consultant to the ACPRA management study team. During his career, Dr. Heneman has served higher education as professor, administrator and consultant. He is now a consultant to Cresap, McCormick and Paget, to the Academy for Educational Development and to other organizations.

Preface

This book concerns itself solely with the management—planning, implementing and evaluating—of programs and activities expressly designed to advance the understanding and support of institutions of higher education. It is written for governing board members, chief executive officers, and key administrators of America's colleges and universities.

The content is based on an extensive study conducted over a period of three years and deals with performance information of the 1962-68 period. It has been augmented by experience gained from on-campus interviews and conversations with leading practitioners and consultants in college management.

The American College Public Relations Association wishes first to express its gratitude to the Esso Educational Foundation, whose grant made this undertaking possible. Thanks are particularly owed to George Buckingham and Frederick deW. Bolman for their helpful counsel and faith in the project.

Next, Charles Newton, assistant to the president of the California Institute of Technology, and Annette L. Bacon, of the development office at the same institution, deserve special acknowledgment for their work in developing the questionnaire, in directing the statistical analysis of the study, and in determining many of the indicators and guidelines described in Chapter II. Miss Bacon also compiled the salary and staff analysis for the years 1964-65 and 1967-68. Appreciation is also gratefully expressed to James M. Shea, formerly director of university relations at the University of Oregon and now a vice president at Temple University, for administering the pilot questionnaire; and to Parry D. Sorensen, assistant to the president at the University of Utah, for visiting schools and compiling reports on campus interviews related to the study. H. Russell Bintzer, Patrick J. Nicholson, Francis C. Pray and Michael Radock contributed their valuable suggestions and services on a number of occasions during the course of the study.

The management consulting firm of Cresap, McCormick and Paget provided expert guidance throughout the study. Harlow J. Heneman, who actively participated in the 1958 Greenbrier Conference, was with the project from the beginning and provided invaluable assistance as did Leo Kornfeld of the same firm.

Finally, the Association is deeply grateful to the hundreds of colleges and universities which participated in this project by painstakingly completing the questionnaire and answering the many follow-up requests for additional details. Without their interest and generous cooperation, the study would not have been possible.

In response to the numerous requests for information which have come as a result of the release of some of the preliminary findings, ACPRA will continue on an annual basis to collect and compile evaluative information and data about institutional advancement programs. It is anticipated that results of its on-going study will be released periodically. An important long-term objective will be to test indicators and evaluative criteria tentatively established by this study.

JOHN W. LESLIE

CHAPTER I

In the Beginning

A. NEED FOR AN ANALYSIS

Higher education was hardly over a period of tremendous expansion strain following World War II when it was faced with even more critical pressures caused by an exploding population, a larger percentage of people requiring a college education, and increased demands for services and research on the part of governments and business.

Higher education has experienced two feast-to-famine cycles in the past 25 years. The country's colleges and universities have managed to survive the strains caused by a dearth of students, materials, and equipment of the war years and the period following the last of the G.I. Bill students in the early fifties; likewise, they have managed somehow to expand in facilities and programs to meet the surges of G.I.'s in 1946 and of "war-babies" beginning in the late 1950's and early 1960's.

It is small wonder then that funding of higher education has multiplied in scope far beyond the modest appropriations of state legislatures and equally modest philanthropic support of pre-war years. The efforts to advance the understanding and support of educational programs have created whole new administrative departments in many institutions and expanded greatly the roles of the relatively few people involved in the activity prior to World War II. Public relations in colleges established itself as a management concept and alumni fund raising efforts broadened into total institutional development programs. However, in-depth analysis of the operation of such programs and the

1

establishment of evaluative criteria were generally of secondary importance to getting the job done.

A dollar pinch is developing for higher education. The 1970's will bring larger student bodies (although they are not expected to continue to increase at the current rate), greater demand for services and research, and continued rapidly rising costs. Competition for the education dollar will become acute. Budgets will be squeezed and all aspects of higher education will have to become more effective and efficient. The challenge to programs and personnel devoted to the furtherance of understanding and financial support will be equally as great. Interpretation of the educational program will be increasingly difficult as institutions grow more complex and the public more sophisticated. Added demands are being placed on the tax dollar and education will find other agencies competing strongly for funds in the state houses and on Capitol Hill. Private wealth is still abundant, but greater breakthroughs in philanthropic motivation will have to be made if education is to obtain the required financing. Combined with the pressures just mentioned is the ever-present reality of rising costs. Just to stay even in the future, the management of educational fund raising and public relations programs will have to be improved greatly in both efficiency and effectiveness.

B. THE GREENBRIER CONFERENCE

Efforts have been made during the past two decades to improve the management of institutional development and public relations programs. The need for long-range planning and the techniques for developing a 10-year budget have been expounded. The refinement and application of more effective communication and fund raising techniques have been at the heart of many a meeting of professional and educational associations.

One such noteworthy conference was held at the Greenbrier Hotel in March 1958. The discussion focused on organizational procedures in the area of public relations, fund raising, and alumni relations programs. A publication, entitled *The Advancement of Understanding and Support of Higher Education* (see Related Readings), reported that the consensus of the conferees favored a unified organizational approach with one officer reporting directly to the president and being responsible for the coordination and direction of the three activities. The report indicated that, while only a fifth of the institutions had such an organizational structure, the vast majority (86.4%) favored this arrangement.

C. The Institutional Advancement Concept

The term "institutional advancement program" or just "advancement program" is employed in this report as a literary and professional convenience and is meant to be applied to the total program implemented by the institution to advance the understanding and support of its educational objectives. Establishing the word "advancement" is not important (a better one may evolve), but implanting the concept is. The advancement program is an umbrella concept typically including public relations activities, alumni programs, fund raising, publications production, and, in some institutions, state and federal liaison, student recruitment, university press operation, central printing and mailing services—to mention a few.

The advancement program is a staff arm of the president to be used by him to develop understanding and support for his and his institution's educational goals. It also is an operating unit with respect to the functions which are included within it.

The advancement concept—coordinated direction and management—is older than the term. The word "development" was originally intended to describe this same concept, but through misuse and misapplication it has tended to become synonymous with fund raising. While vital, fund raising is only one of the purposes of the institutional advancement program. Gift support—the by-product of fund raising— is also only one of the means to finance higher education. Tuitions, appropriations, federal grants, endowments, and auxiliary enterprises combine with gifts to support colleges and universities. Each source varies in importance among institutions, but each must be examined carefully for its potential in playing an important role in financial management.

An institution's advancement program, just as its financial management operations, is the implementation of a broad concept. The management study discussed in this report analyzed the four principal activities—information services, fund raising, alumni relations, and publications—constituting the chief areas of responsibility of most executive officers charged with the management of the advancement program. In some cases these officers direct the state and federal liaison activities, but if not, they make sure both areas are coordinated with advancement activities. The advancement program manager is also vitally concerned with his institution's academic programs, student relationships, and business operations. Like the other executive officers, he serves the president with information, counsel, and effective action on the part of the departments under him.

D. THE MANAGEMENT STUDY

The need to develop better management procedures and evaluative criteria prompted the Board of Trustees of the American College Public Relations Association (ACPRA) in 1965 to commission a management study of the broad educational advancement field. The study encompasses statistics from the 1962-63 through the 1967-68 school years.

Specific objectives of the study were:

• To obtain information regarding present administrative practices employed in college advancement programs.

• To provide college presidents and administrators with up-to-date and objective knowledge about present organization, evaluative criteria, methods and trends in institutional advancement programs.

• To make a beginning in the improvement and clarification of financial and program reporting within higher education, particularly regarding fund raising, by attempting to establish certain norms, methods, and standard terminology.

• To provide advancement programs with objective standards and criteria not limited to the educational field but incorporating data drawn from the opinions and practices of corporations, foundations and other institutions.

• Finally, to identify and make available to the degree possible to higher education the most effective administrative organization, procedures, staffing and management practices.

E. Conducting the Study

In addition to a thorough search of the literature, the study used questionnaires and personal interviews to gather information.

Several questionnaires were mailed to accredited institutions of higher education; the principal one entitled, "New Trends in Public Relations and Fund Raising at U.S. Colleges and Universities" (see Appendix A), was sent to 1,200 such institutions. Approximately 700 replies were received. They were reviewed for completeness and comparability, and a supplemental questionnaire was sent out to 445 institutions in order to clarify certain budgetary data. From the response to both questionnaires, 105 institutions which provided usable and comparable data were selected for the study analysis. These 105 were deemed to be representative of four-year institutions of higher education (excluding state colleges) and were composed of the following:

State Universities	19
Private Universities	12
Private Coed Colleges	56
Private Men's Colleges	8
Private Women's Colleges	10
	105

A preliminary report of the questionnaire findings was prepared and circulated to selected university and college presidents. At the same time, interviews—with presidents, deans, faculty, and administrative officers—were conducted at a representative sample of institutions to double-check responses and to amplify the information received.

F. The Report

The questionnaires, the interviews, the literature, the studies of specific institutions, the thinking of individuals participating in the study, as well as the ideas of experienced persons in the field were analyzed and evaluated. The result is this report which relates the results of the study, suggests criteria for evaluation of advancement programs, and discusses organizational processes and patterns.

This report is designed for the members of the governing board and the chief executive officers of the institution. Administrative officers primarily responsible for some portion of the institution's advancement program undoubtedly will find it helpful and informative, but the report is not intended to discuss limited professional, philosophical, and technical questions of interest solely to advancement program personnel.

CHAPTER II

Study Findings: Present Status of Advancement Programs in Higher Education

America's colleges and universities receive between $1.5 and $2 billion in gift support, and gift income has more than doubled in the past 10 years. But in spite of the sharp increase and large sums involved, few objective and quantitative criteria to measure the success of advancement programs have been made available to serve as a guide to the college president. Decisions have tended to be made on what Walter Lippmann called the pseudo-environment, the imagined environment the person places between himself and the real world.

Reasons for the lack of meaningful performance data are many and complex.

• Since educational institutions do not have the profit motive of the commercial enterprise, they have tended to be more casual in their accounting and management practices.

• Definitive allocation of resources—staff and funds—is just beginning to occur.

• The entire advancement field is relatively new to higher education and has experienced spectacular growth during the past two decades.

• Imprecise performance data among institutions are the result of varying job descriptions and definitions of what constitutes gift income.

Combine all of these factors with the promotional flair which affects the arithmetic of some college presidents and public relations

7

and development officers and one can appreciate the problems inherent in analyzing the educational advancement field.

Important selected findings from the 105-institution study are presented in this chapter. The discussion and guidelines of chapters III and IV are based upon these findings and upon interview-data with institutions and professionals in the field. The information obtained from analysis of the study data gives answers to many significant questions, including the following:

- How are advancement program activities commonly organized?

- What are the sizes of professional staffs of advancement programs, and what are their salaries?

- What are some promising possible yardsticks and evaluative criteria for measuring fund raising effectiveness?

- What efforts and expenditures are being allocated to advancement programs, and what are some of the results?

A. Organizational Structure

1. *The Centralized Approach to Managing the Advancement Program*

All institutions of higher education engage in fund raising, public relations, and alumni activities. The extent of involvement in these various activities depends to some degree upon size, traditions, present and past leadership, and historical accident. However, any implementation of such activities requires some sort of organizational structure.

The study found that there are four main activities or functions commonly identified with the overall advancement program: fund raising, information services, publications, and alumni relations. Other related activities such as federal and/or state liaison, university presses, central printing services, student recruitment, job placement of graduates, and educational television, are, to varying degrees, considered by a number of institutions to fall within the organizational scope of the advancement program. In most cases, activities of this kind are handled by staff people considered to be operating within one of the four broad functions.

Before considering the organizational structure two points having to do with functions and job titles should be kept in mind. First, in delineating the various functions within the advancement program, the number of functions must not be confused with either the numbers or offices of people. For example, in many institutions, publications production is part of the information services office, and sometimes fund raising and alumni relations offices are combined. Furthermore, there may be any number of professional people within one of the offices, or one person may perform two functions.

Secondly, titles tend to be meaningless in determining level of authority of the manager of the advancement program at different institutions. Although "vice president" is the most common title, there are directors, deans, and assistants to the president who act as chief directing and coordinating officers for the advancement program. Of 64 advancement program managers in the 105 institutions in the study sample, 30 were vice presidents. Since a director of development and a vice president for university relations may have comparable positions in different institutions, functional definitions, rather than titles, were used in the study.

In conducting the programs connected with fund raising, information services, publications, and alumni relations, a centralized management approach was frequently used. The study found that the alignment of at least three of the four main activities under one manager was the most common organization pattern. In the study sample of 105 representative institutions the breakdown for 1964-65, when the first questionnaire was used, was as follows:

TABLE 1

Centrally Managed Advancement Programs in 1964-65

	State Universities	Private Universities	Private Colleges
One officer reporting to president	56%	75%	61%
More than one officer reporting to president	44%	25%	39%
	100%	100%	100%

A follow-up analysis of organizational structure and salaries was made for 1967-68, and will be covered in greater detail later in this chapter's discussion of professional staffs and salaries.

An analysis of data obtained from the 1967-68 sample, which included 378 institutions, indicated a small but distinct increase in the number of centrally managed advancement programs between 1964-65 and 1967-68 (see Table 2). It should be noted that the institutional composition of the 1967-68 salary study sample differed from the 105 sample used in the main study in that the former included state colleges. Notably, in each category of institutional type in the 378 sample, the trend was toward a centralized organizational structure in advancement programs. The exceptions were the state colleges and private women's colleges, for fewer than half of them were thus organized. As yet advancement programs are in an embryonic stage in many state colleges. The majority of state colleges (55 percent) conducted only one advancement program activity—public relations—and, therefore, needed no overall manager. Furthermore, less than one-fourth of these institutions had a full-time person specially assigned to fund raising. The comparison between the data for 1964-65 and 1967-68 showed an eight percent increase, from 39 to 47 percent, in the number of centrally managed advancement programs. Excluding state colleges, the percentages would be 46 and 56 percent.

In a questionnaire survey made in 1957, prior to the Greenbrier Conference, it was found that 20 percent of the responding institutions had a single coordinating officer reporting directly to the president. Clearly the trend over the past 10 years has been toward the centralized organizational pattern. Other than the centralized management approach, no particular organizational pattern tends to get wide utilization. However, a number of institutions have all advancement functions reporting directly to the chief executive officer, such as the president or chancellor. Others split the public relations and development responsibilities between two vice presidents or directors.

2. Organizational Patterns by Type of Institution

An examination of the type of organizational structure used by different kinds of institutions may suggest trends as well as whether certain patterns are suited to certain kinds of institutions. As the following material shows, there are some distinct differences between state and private universities, and between private universities and private colleges.

TABLE 2

Growth in Centralized Advancement Program Management between 1964-65 and 1967-68

Type of Institution	Number of Institutions Reporting for 1964-65 and 1967-68	Number with Single Managers in 1964-65	Lost	Gained	Number with Single Managers in 1967-68	Percent with Single Managers in 1967-68
Private Universities	21	15	0	2	17	81%
Private Coed Colleges	165	81	4	17	94	57
Private Men's Colleges	28	14	1	7	20	71
Private Women's Colleges	42	11	1	4	14	34
State Universities	42	18	1	4	21	50
State Colleges	80	10	2	4	12	15
Totals	378	149	9	38	178	47%

State Universities

Of the 105 responding institutions comprising the study sample, 19 were state universities. In regard to the line of command for advancement program activities, two basic organizational structures were in evidence, the first occurring in 10 of the 19 state universities:

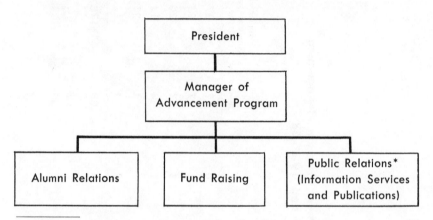

* Public relations in this and other charts in the chapter includes information services and publications. In some institutions these activities are split, with each office reporting separately to the manager.

In this structure, a single officer was responsible for the entire program and reported to the president. In five of these 10 universities, the officer had the title of vice president, while in the remaining five, he was called director or assistant to the president.

A second basic organizational structure, found in five state universities, divided advancement program activities into two broad functions, one being public relations and the other a combination of fund raising and alumni relations. These two functions reported separately to the president:

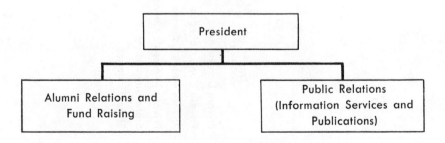

The remaining four state universities used variations of this second, less centralized organizational structure. At two state universities, components of the advancement program were handled by three officers reporting to the president. At one university, fund raising reported directly to the president, while alumni relations and public relations were coordinated by an administrative dean. The one remaining state university had all four functions reporting directly to the president.

Among the recent trends noted in the advancement programs at state universities are:

• a strong tendency toward centralizing the various advancement program activities under a single manager who reports directly to the president,

• the inclusion of the manager of the advancement program (whatever his title) in the top decision-making and policy-making group,

• the increasing use of the title "vice president" for the manager of an institution's advancement program, and

• expansion of fund raising activities and staffs as private funds are increasingly sought.

Private Universities

Twelve of the 105 respondents in the sample were private universities. Nine of these 12 had a single officer at the vice president level who managed the advancement program. Within the nine centralized programs two different organizational structures were noted, the first being found in seven of the universities:

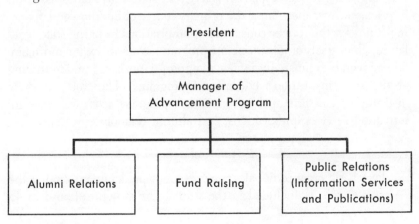

The centrally managed programs at two other private universities were organized similarly, except that fund raising and alumni relations were combined.

At the remaining three institutions, a single manager for the advancement program did not exist. In two institutions, the advancement program was separated into two functions, each of which reported to the president. One function, fund raising, was headed by a vice president in both institutions, while the other function, a combined public relations and alumni relations office, was headed by a vice president in one university and a director in the second:

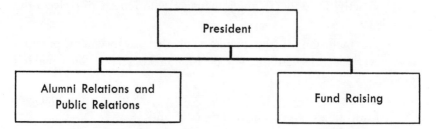

At the remaining university, the organization was similar to the one above, except that alumni relations was a separate function, while fund raising and public relations were combined.

As in the state universities, the manager of the centrally organized advancement program in most of these private institutions was titled "vice president," and also the trend is for him to become increasingly involved in overall university decision-making at the top management level. However, a difference should be noted at this point. Fund raising was not as highly developed an activity in state universities as it was in private universities. Since the primary source of building and operating funds for the former consists of appropriations from the state legislature, chief goals of advancement programs were to create and maintain a favorable climate for increased appropriations and understanding of the state institution's educational programs. Therefore, at these institutions, the principal advancement program activities were information services, publications, and alumni relations.

Private Colleges

Two basic organizational structures were predominant among the 74 private colleges included in the study. The structure found in 45 colleges had a director or vice president managing the advancement program as follows:

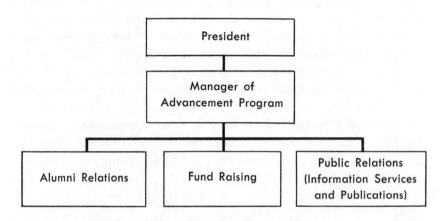

Variations of this structure at some colleges separated the advancement program into one or two functions reporting to the managing officer. For example, 11 of the colleges used an officer to coordinate two functions, with the officer himself handling the third function, usually fund raising. Six colleges had only one function—public relations—staffed below the manager level, with the managing officer presumably handling fund raising and alumni relations himself. In one college, one staff member was responsible for handling all advancement program functions.

The second basic less centralized structure, found in 24 colleges, had the three main advancement functions reporting directly to the president:

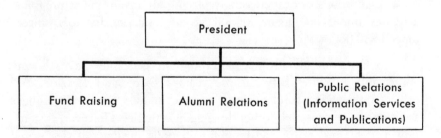

A variation of this structure was used by the five remaining colleges, where two officers reported directly to the president.

In comparing the trends toward the centralized organization approach, it was noted that well over half of the private colleges had a chief managing officer, thus falling on a scale between the state universities in which slightly over half had this arrangement, and the private universities in which three-fourths of the institutions utilized this centralized organizational structure. Private colleges with a single manager varied according to the type of college; for coed colleges it was 57 percent, for men's colleges, 71 percent, and for women's colleges it was 34 percent. In the private college, the manager of the advancement program, even if his title were vice president, was not typically involved in key decisions affecting the institution. Instead, he generally tended to become involved at the point where implementation was needed.

B. Size and Salaries of Advancement Program Professional Staffs

Professional staffs of advancement programs and their salaries were analyzed for the two budget years, 1964-65 and 1967-68. The 1964-65 figures drew upon the sample study of 105 institutions, while the 1967-68 survey analyzed data on professional staff and salaries from 378 institutions. All salary figures cited exclude fringe benefits. Some of the highlights of the analysis were:

• Private universities tended to have the largest advancement program staffs—with a median of 14 professionals. State universities had a median of 10 to 11 professionals on their advancement program staffs, and private college staffs ranged from three to five professionals.

• Institutions were increasingly placing all advancement program activities under one managing officer, and salaries for this officer topped $30,000.

• Salaries for all advancement program personnel have shown appreciable increases between the years 1964-65 and 1967-68. At private universities, fund raising personnel tended to receive higher salaries than persons in the other three main activities. However, at state universities fund raising and public relations median salaries were about the same, with alumni relations and publications following, in that order.

Detailed statistical information supporting these findings is given in Appendix B, and the discussion below is intended only as a summary.

1. Advancement Program Staff Sizes

The survey for the 1967-68 budget year found that a total of 2,095 professional staff personnel were directly involved in advancement activities at 378 institutions. The number and type of institutions comprising the sample were as follows:

Private Universities	21
Private Coed Colleges	165
Private Men's Colleges	28
Private Women's Colleges	42
State Universities	42
State Colleges	80
	378

The 378 institutions in the sample were deemed to be representative of four-year institutions of higher learning, and the distribution by type is generally consistent with the institutional diversity within higher education, excluding junior colleges.

Private universities generally have the largest advancement program staffs, the median being 14 for the 21 institutions in the sample. State college staffs tend to be smallest, with some colleges having only one person. The staff medians drawn from Table 2 in Appendix B were:

Private Universities	14
Private Coed Colleges	4-5
Private Men's Colleges	5
Private Women's Colleges	3-4
State Universities	10-11
State Colleges	2-3

Based on additional analysis of the 1967-68 data, it is interesting to note that while all private universities had fund raising staffs, such was not the case with private colleges. Nineteen percent of the coed colleges, four percent of the men's colleges, and 43 percent of the women's colleges had no fund raising staff designated as such. It is surmised that what fund raising was done was probably conducted by the alumni office staff and by the president and others.

Emphasis at state institutions was clearly on public relations activities. All of the 42 universities and 80 colleges had public relations staffs, but only 72 percent of the universities and 24 percent of the colleges indicated having designated fund raising persons (see Appendix B, Table 1). Ninety percent of the state universities had chief alumni officers, while less than half (45 percent) of the state colleges had comparable personnel.

The 63 state and private universities displayed a much larger spread in staff size than existed between the state and private colleges. Staffs ranged from seven to more than 25 in the private universities and from two to 22 in the state universities. The private colleges tended to be fairly well clustered in the three to five staff member range, while two-thirds of the state colleges were in the one to three staff member range.

2. *Salary Analysis*

Salary information was provided on all 2,095 professional positions in the 1967-68 analysis of advancement program staffs. Some positions were indicated as temporarily vacant but the budget allocation figure was given. Figures were straight salary with no fringe benefits included.

Salaries ranged beyond $30,000 for managers of the advancement program and into the upper twenties for chief fund raising officers (see Appendix B, Tables 3A to 3F). The median for 17 persons responsible for managing the total program in their respective private universities was in the $25,000-$29,999 range. Their counterparts in state universities were a notch below, in the $20,000-$24,999 bracket.

In all but state and private women's colleges, the salary median for the persons responsible for managing the advancement program was two brackets (at least $5,000) above the median for this highest paid subordinate chief of any of the four principal advancement program functions. In women's colleges, however, the separation was one bracket, while at state colleges the medians for chief fund raising officers and advancement program managers were the same.

3. *Salary Increases between 1964-65 and 1967-68*

Using the data for two budget years, a comparison of salaries was made for advancement program managers and chief officers of the four principal functions (see Appendix B, Tables 4A to 4F). Managers of advancement programs increased their salaries, with the majority moving into the $25,000 to $29,999 range, which less than half of them had occupied three years before. Most of the medians for the chief officers jumped one salary bracket (i.e., $2,500) over the three-year span. Exceptions were the medians for fund raising chiefs in state universities, which moved two steps upward to the $15,000 to $17,499 range. The same jump was made in the medians for chief public relations officers in women's colleges.

C. YARDSTICKS FOR MEASURING FUND RAISING EFFECTIVENESS

The findings discussed thus far deal with the organizational structure of advancement program activities and with the size of staffs and salaries paid. Both are of interest in suggesting the variations in an institution's commitment and approach to advancing the understanding and support of its educational objectives. While these data shed some light on the means, what is of far greater concern are the results of advancement programs. The data presented in the next part of the chapter are just the beginning of an effort to come to grips with the important questions of effectiveness and efficiency. To measure the outcomes of advancement programs, yardsticks capable of determining performance are needed. In the analysis of data collected for this study, various possible yardsticks are considered.

1. *Gift Income and its Relation to Total Gifts*

The definition of voluntary support used in the study is the one developed by the Council for Financial Aid to Education (CFAE). Voluntary support or total gifts includes: cash or securities; new additions to existing funds, but not earned income; donated real property valued as carried on the institution's books; book value of annuities and life income contracts; and the cash value of life insurance contracts owned by the institution. Not included in total gifts are federal, state, or local government appropriations or grants, unpaid balances on pledges, or bequest expectancies.

Total gifts include gifts for both current and capital purposes. Obviously, total gift income is what the institution is ultimately interested in, and certainly total gift income over a long period of time —10, 20, or 30 years—is a reflection of an institution's long-term advancement program performance. However, results over a long period of time do not necessarily give an adequate picture of current performance; yet it is current performance that suggests whether there are flaws in the fund raising program which must be corrected. What gift income figures should then be used? Total gift income for one year can be distorted by one unusually large gift, such as a bequest; but five years may be too long a period to measure because of rapid growth and evolution in higher education. Clearly a compromise is needed to provide figures which are relatively up-to-date and relatively undistorted.

For this study, therefore, an average of three years, 1962-63, 1964-65, and 1965-66, was used for gift income and expenditures. For this relatively short period, the inclusion of deferred gifts—life income agreements and trusts, bequests, gift annuities, and insurance policies —would have distorted the picture because (1) such gifts do not necessarily reflect current effort (especially bequests), and (2) their year-to-year receipt by an institution can be erratic. For this reason, a three-year average of *gift income exclusive of deferred gifts* was used in the study, as this figure tends to eliminate short-term fluctuations and more nearly represents today's gifts resulting from today's work.

An initial important finding of the study was to confirm that gift income exclusive of deferred gifts constitutes a reliable index of total gifts as Chart A indicates. According to CFAE figures, gifts exclusive of deferred gifts in the nation as a whole averaged about 83 percent of total gifts for the three gift-income years. The average of the study sample is 90 percent, which is slightly higher. Chart A illustrates the correlation between rank standing in total gifts and rank standing in gifts exclusive of deferred gifts. It may be seen that the institutions getting the greatest amount of outright gifts also receive the greatest amount of total gifts. Examining Chart A, one finds there is an excellent correlation. The rank standing of the 105 institutions arranged in order of ascending size of total gifts is almost the same as when they are arranged in order of gifts exclusive of deferred gifts. The index of

CHART A

CORRELATION BETWEEN RANK STANDING IN TOTAL GIFTS AND
RANK STANDING IN GIFTS EXCLUSIVE OF DEFERRED GIFTS

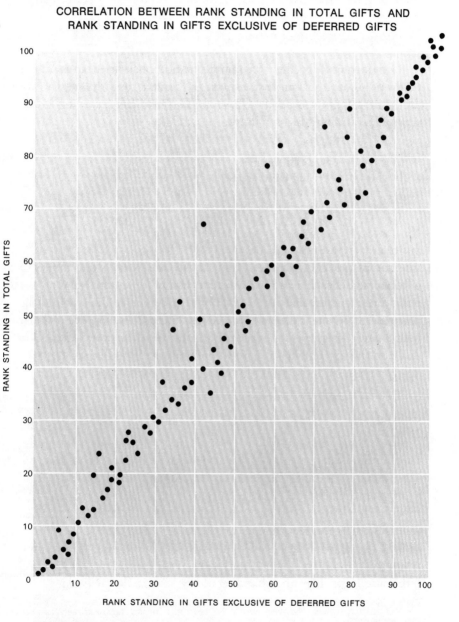

RANK STANDING IN GIFTS EXCLUSIVE OF DEFERRED GIFTS

105 Institutions t/σ = 13.8   ● = One Institution

Tau over sigma (t/σ) is an index of rank correlation developed by M. G. Kendall. The larger the correlation figure, the closer are two sets of data when arranged in order of size. When the value is between plus 2 and minus 2, rank correlations are insignificant. A large *negative* value indicates close *inverse* correlation.

rank correlation is 13.8, a correlation so high that it would occur by chance less than once in a million times. Therefore, gifts exclusive of deferred gifts offer a good yardstick for total fund raising performance.

2. *Gift Income Analyzed by Type of Institution*

Gift income* for the 105 sample institutions varied from under $100,000 to over $10 million, as seen in Chart B, and the median for the entire sample was about $700,000. The medians according to the type of institution are as follows:

State Universities	$ 850,000
Private Universities	$3,650,000
Private Coed Colleges	$ 550,000
Private Men's Colleges	$ 750,000
Private Women's Colleges	$ 550,000

An examination of Chart B will reveal the distributions and ranges of gift income for each type of institution. It should be noted that all the private universities had received gifts of over one million, while the majority of private colleges received less than a million. Top dollar figures are represented by one state institution with over $10 million and one private university with approximately $9 million.

3. *Expenditures for Advancement Programs*

As in the computation of gift income, the study used averages for the same three years—1962-63, 1964-65, and 1965-66—in determining expenditures for institutional advancement programs. To repeat, advancement is the umbrella term for the program which includes fund raising, information services, publications, and alumni relations. Although not all the institutions studied have these activities organized into four separate departments or offices, all have their expenditures broken down in such a way that costs of fund raising and alumni relations, on the one hand, and costs of information services and publications, on the other hand, could be separately analyzed.

---

* Hereafter, unless otherwise noted, the term gift income means three-year averages of gifts exclusive of deferred gifts.

CHART B

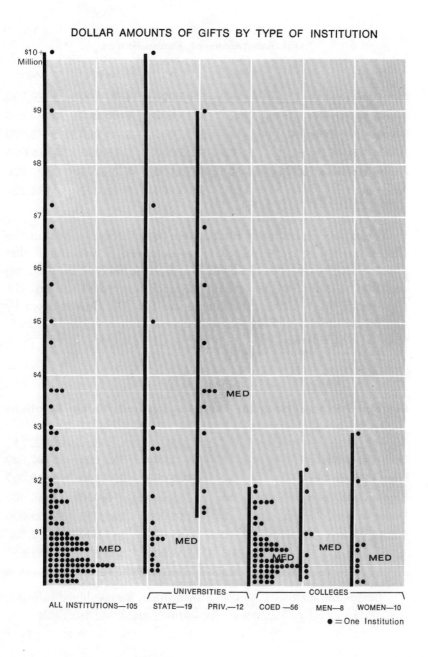

DOLLAR AMOUNTS OF GIFTS BY TYPE OF INSTITUTION

● = One Institution

The ranges and medians of total advancement expenditures, according to type of institution, are as follows:

TABLE 3

Total Advancement Expenditures

	Number	High	Low	Median
State Universities	19	$535,000	$ 75,000	$220,000
Private Universities	12	$715,000	$185,000	$395,000
Private Coed Colleges	56	$305,000	$ 25,000	$ 95,000
Private Men's Colleges	8	$215,000	$ 75,000	$145,000
Private Women's Colleges	10	$275,000	$ 35,000	$120,000
All Institutions	105	$715,000	$ 25,000	$125,000

When the expenditures for the four major activities within the advancement program were separately examined, it was found that private universities, as would be expected, spent more on fund raising and alumni relations. The median for fund raising and alumni relations for all institutions in the sample was $75,000. Broken down by type of institution, the ranges and medians for the combined expenditures were as follows:

TABLE 4

Combined Expenditures for Fund Raising and Alumni Relations

	Number	High	Low	Median
State Universities	19	$415,000	$15,000	$ 85,000
Private Universities	12	$445,000	$95,000	$265,000
Private Coed Colleges	56	$235,000	$ 5,000	$ 60,000
Private Men's Colleges	8	$155,000	$35,000	$105,000
Private Women's Colleges	10	$255,000	$15,000	$ 85,000
All Institutions	105	$445,000	$ 5,000	$ 75,000

Ranges and medians, by type of institution, for combined information services and publications expenditures are listed in Table 5.

CHART C

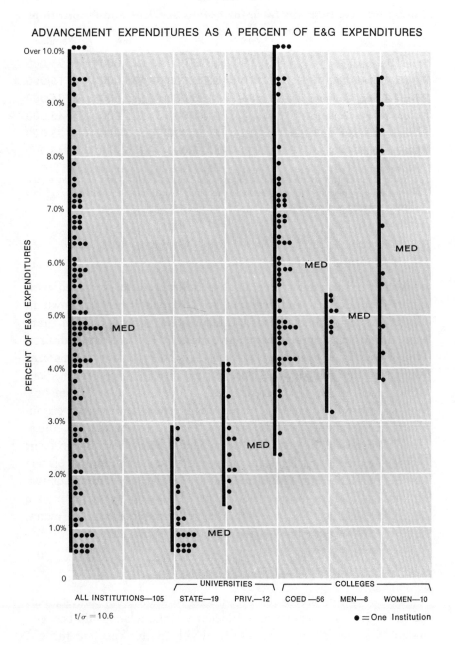

ADVANCEMENT EXPENDITURES AS A PERCENT OF E&G EXPENDITURES

TABLE 5

Combined Expenditures for Information Services and Publications

	Number	High	Low	Median
State Universities	19	$325,000	$45,000	$125,000
Private Universities	12	$275,000	$75,000	$115,000
Private Coed Colleges	56	$135,000	$ 5,000	$ 35,000
Private Men's Colleges	8	$ 75,000	$25,000	$ 45,000
Private Women's Colleges	10	$ 55,000	$15,000	$ 35,000
All Institutions	105	$325,000	$ 5,000	$ 45,000

Note: The high, low and median figures in Tables 4 and 5 will not add to the corresponding figures in Table 3, because the same institutions are not high and low in Tables 4 and 5.

4. *Advancement Program Expenditures Compared with E&G Expenditures*

When advancement program expenditures were compared with the total educational and general (E&G) expenditures, as shown in Chart C, it was observed that the median for advancement program expenditures was approximately five percent of E&G expenditures. Universities, public and private, were generally below two percent whereas private colleges were close to a five and a half percent median, with a wide range of difference both above and below. State universities not only spent less money than private universities on advancement programs, but also spent a smaller portion of their educational and general budgets on advancement. The median advancement program expenditure for state universities was eight-tenths of one percent, while private universities had a median expenditure of two and one-half percent of the E&G budget. The medians for the private colleges were almost six percent for the coed, five percent for the men's, and over six and one-half percent for the women's colleges.

5. *Fund Raising Efficiency and Effectiveness*

Efficiency and effectiveness have somewhat different connotations, but there is a close relationship. Efficiency is the relationship between resources expended and the results, which in this case are the gift incomes that are received. Effectiveness is a measurement of the de-

CHART D

COST OF GIFTS PER DOLLAR RAISED

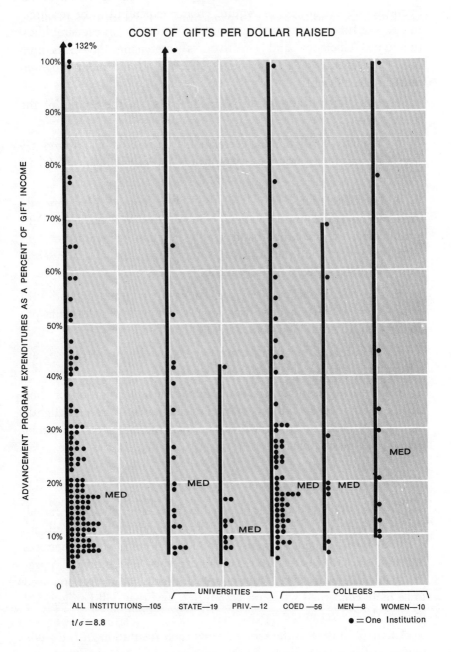

ADVANCEMENT PROGRAM EXPENDITURES AS A PERCENT OF GIFT INCOME

UNIVERSITIES

COLLEGES

ALL INSTITUTIONS—105   STATE—19   PRIV.—12   COED—56   MEN—8   WOMEN—10

$t/\sigma = 8.8$

● = One Institution

gree to which objectives are successfully achieved. Obviously some financial support objectives require greater expenditures of resources in terms of funds and staff than do others. It may be an oversimplification to use "efficiency" and "effectiveness" interchangeably—as is often done. However, over a long period, effective advancement programs must also be efficient.

Several generalizations can be made based on the results of the study:

• A relatively high rank correlation $(t/\sigma = 8.8)$ was found between advancement program expenditures and gift dollars (see Chart E).

• The correlation became slightly higher $(t/\sigma = 9.1)$ when only fund raising and alumni relations expenditures were matched with gift income; on the other hand, public relations expenditures (information services and publications) showed much less of a correlation with gift dollars (see Charts F and G).

• The cost of raising funds, advancement program expenditures as a percent of gift income, was approximately 15 to 20 cents per dollar with a wide range both ways (Chart D).

• As an institution raises more money, its advancement program expenditures per gift dollar decrease (Chart I).

• Private institutions which allocated the larger portion of their advancement program budgets to fund raising tended to receive slightly more gift dollars than those which allocated the larger part to public relations activities (Chart J).

Cost per Dollar Raised

To determine as accurately as possible the cost per gift dollar raised, the study compared advancement program expenditures with gift income. Obviously, there are many non-budgeted items, such as services of presidents and trustees and overhead expenses, which do not appear in the advancement expenditure figures. Educational institutions need to be more concerned with cost accounting, but that will be discussed in more detail later in the report.

Chart D illustrates the cost in cents each institution in the study sample spent to raise each dollar. On Chart D, each dot represents

CHART E

ADVANCEMENT PROGRAM EXPENDITURES COMPARED WITH
GIFT INCOME RECEIVED

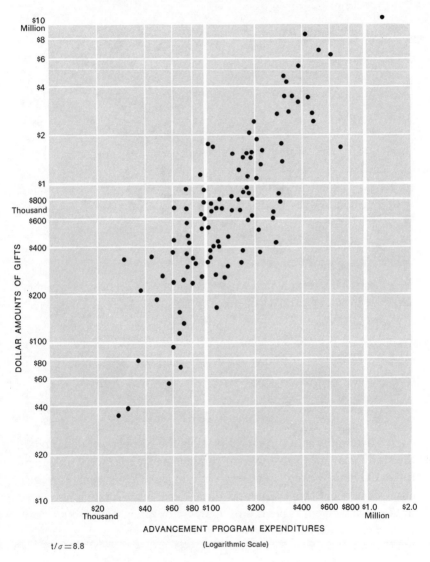

DOLLAR AMOUNTS OF GIFTS

ADVANCEMENT PROGRAM EXPENDITURES

$t/\sigma = 8.8$

(Logarithmic Scale)

CHART F

RELATING FUND RAISING AND ALUMNI EXPENDITURES TO GIFTS

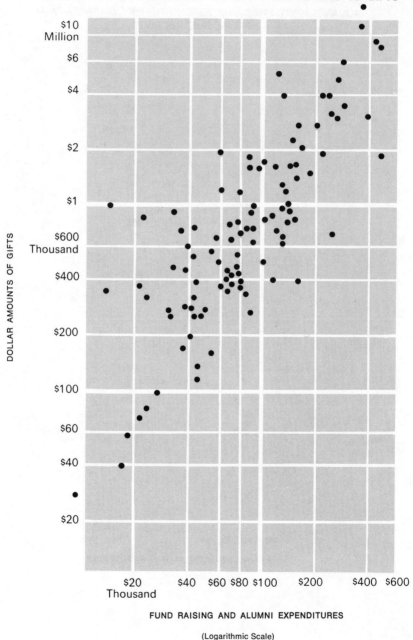

DOLLAR AMOUNTS OF GIFTS

FUND RAISING AND ALUMNI EXPENDITURES

(Logarithmic Scale)

t/σ = 9.1

● = One Institution

CHART G

RELATING INFORMATION AND PUBLICATIONS EXPENDITURES TO GIFTS

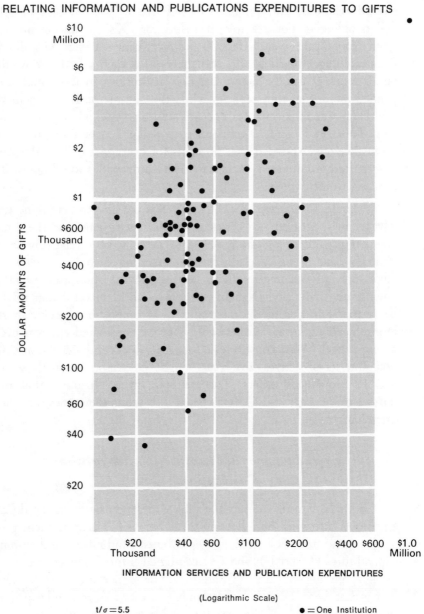

DOLLAR AMOUNTS OF GIFTS

INFORMATION SERVICES AND PUBLICATION EXPENDITURES

(Logarithmic Scale)

$t/\sigma = 5.5$ ● = One Institution

one institution plotted vertically according to the percentage it expends for its total advancement program—fund raising, information services, alumni relations, and publications—relative to the number of gift dollars obtained. For example, if Institution "X's" advancement program expenditures were $100,000 and its gift income were $1 million, the percentage would be 10, and the cost of each gift dollar would be 10 cents. It will be noted that two institutions in the sample expended more than they took in, while the cost of the least expensive gift dollar was four cents for one private university. Most institutions spent between 15 and 20 cents for each dollar, but over one of every 10 institutions expended over 50 cents for every gift dollar. Medians ranged from a low of 11 cents for private universities to a high of 25 cents for women's colleges.

It should be realized that the study was not able to determine the advancement program objectives of specific institutions, and the three one-year periods of the study, 1962 to 1966, were a relatively short period of time. For certain objectives, expending almost as much as or more than gift income might be justified in the short run. On the other hand, while advancement programs with high-cost dollars might be deemed *effective* by the institution in accomplishing specific short-term objectives, by no means could they be considered *efficient* over a long period. What constitutes a long period depends on the institution and its objectives—five years might be reasonable with some, and 10 years with others. The example given illustrates that the terms "efficiency" and "effectiveness" at least sometimes are not interchangeable.

Expenditures for Advancement Program Activities Compared with Gifts

Charts E, F and G depict the rank correlation between the dollar amount of gifts and the following three items: (1) advancement program expenditures (Chart E); (2) combined fund raising and alumni expenditures (Chart F); and (3) combined information services and publications expenditures (Chart G). The important point to note here is that there is a high correlation between gift income and expenditures for each pair of the activities. This high correlation tends to substantiate the belief of many practitioners that information services, publications, alumni activities and fund raising are interdependent. While the first three activities in themselves may raise little money, they each contribute essentially to effective fund raising.

Relationships between Gifts and E&G Expenditures

No clear relationship could be observed when the educational and general expenditures of institutions were correlated with their gift incomes. In other words, as E&G expenditures increase or decrease there is no corresponding pattern of gift dollars increasing or decreasing accordingly. However, when institutions were ranked according to gifts, and this rank-order was projected against gifts as a percent of E&G expenditures, an interesting pattern was established, as shown in Chart H. With the state universities (note the "S's" at left side of the chart), gifts increased along with expenditures, but as a percentage of E&G expenditures they remained relatively constant, with the majority being less than 10 percent of E&G expenditures.

By contrast, both in private universities and colleges, as gift income increased, it became a larger percentage of the institution's E&G expenditures. Several explanations could be ventured for this phenomenon, but all are conjectures. The private institutions at the top of the chart could possibly have become used to a larger proportion of gifts and therefore be reluctant to seek increased funds from other sources such as tuition. Or the reverse could be true—that other sources of funds are considered "over-tapped" and gift dollars provide the only avenue for additional financing of the educational program. Similarly, it could be possible that the private institutions at the bottom portion of Chart H are depending too heavily on tuition, or are not taking full advantage of their fund raising potential. Whatever the reasons, and there are probably several at work in combination, further research would have to be conducted to determine if it is more appropriate for gifts to remain a fairly constant percentage of E&G expenditures or to become a greater portion of E&G expenditures as gift income increases.

Relationships between Gifts and Advancement Program Expenditures

Presidents of institutions of higher learning and their managers of advancement programs constantly face two perplexing questions:

CHART H

GIFT DOLLARS AS A PERCENT OF E&G EXPENDITURES

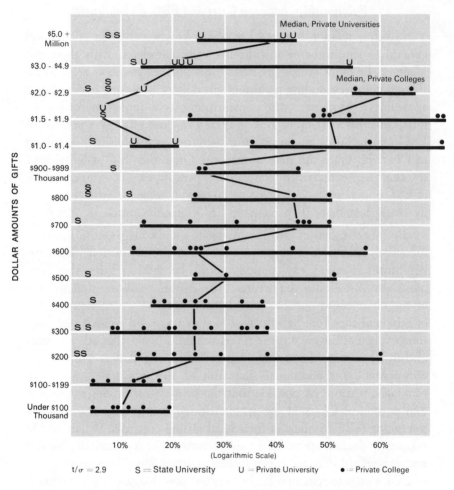

Medians of private colleges and private universities are connected.

• Is there a direct relationship between the amount spent and the gift dollars obtained, i.e., if you spend more, will you receive equivalently more?

• Is there a point of diminishing returns at which gift dollars cost more to raise as gift income increases, i.e., after you have raised a certain amount of money, will the next amounts be harder to raise and thus will the effort cost more?

There are no definite answers to these questions—and there may never be. However, the study data give some interesting indications. The analysis of the 105 institutions in the sample showed generally that the more gift dollars raised, the *less* they *all* cost to raise (Chart I). The solid line which connects the medians continues to move to the left, indicating less average cost per gift dollar as gift income increases. It must be admitted, though, that the cost per gift dollar in Chart I is the average cost, and not the cost of raising "X" amount more, which is the management problem alluded to in the second question above, i.e., if it costs 20 cents on the dollar to raise $5 million, will the allocation of a like amount increase gift income at the same ratio? Presumably there are upper limits which set a ceiling on such efforts. But Chart I indicates that institutions have probably not yet reached a point of diminishing returns for their advancement program expenditures.

It should be noted that nearly all institutions which received $1 million or more in gifts were getting them for less than 20 cents on the dollar, and the same situation prevailed with over two out of three of the institutions which received between a half million and $1 million. On the other hand, no institution whose gifts were less than $200,000 had such low costs; indeed, the median for this group was over 60 cents per gift dollar, and for only one institution was the cost less than 40 cents. Looking at Chart I, one sees that the range for big-gift institutions is quite narrow, and even the state universities which fall into high-gift brackets stay fairly close to the median. At the bottom of the chart the opposite is true and the ranges are great.

As gifts of larger denominations to institutions tend to cost proportionately less to raise than those of smaller amounts, presidents and other persons responsible for managing advancement programs should see from this chart the importance of selective focusing of their insti-

CHART I

ADVANCEMENT PROGRAM CENTS-COST PER GIFT DOLLAR

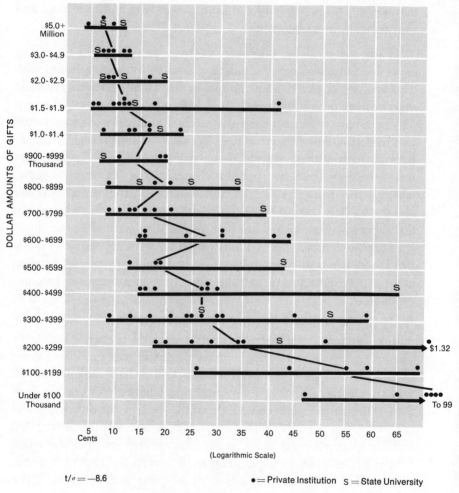

t/σ = —8.6   • = Private Institution   S = State University

Medians of each gift range are connected.

tution's efforts. Still to be researched is the motivational value that small gifts and givers have on large gifts. But it is quite obvious that programs which generally receive a greater portion of "big gifts" are most productive and, therefore, point the way to stretch the institution's available resources.

Relationships between Fund Raising and Alumni Relations Expenditures, and Information Services and Publications Expenditures

Comparing combined fund raising and alumni expenditures with combined expenditures for information services and publications is an oversimplification because, as stated before, all four activities appear to be interdependent upon one another in a successful advancement program. However, it is interesting to look at the allocation of expenditures between the two groups of activities as given in Chart J. State universities spent about one-third of the advancement budget on fund raising and alumni relations—or, stated another way, fund raising and alumni activities received about half the amount expended for information services and publications.

In private institutions, almost the reverse allocation was true— fund raising and alumni relations received the larger share. Furthermore, it appears that as advancement program expenditures increased, the percent allocated to fund raising and alumni also increased. The median for private institutions with advancement expenditures under $50,000 was 50 percent. But as the expenditures increased, fund raising and alumni activities combined received a greater portion, with the medians climbing upward and ranging from 60 percent to over 70 percent. Private institutions which received over $100,000 in gift income allocated about two-thirds of their advancement program expenditures to fund raising and alumni, while private institutions receiving less than $100,000 in gifts allocated somewhat larger percentages to information services and publications and only approximately 50 percent of their expenditures for fund raising and alumni activities.

6. Gift Income and the Alumni

Of all the various advancement program functions, alumni activities are the oldest. In addition, the study found that alumni office

38

CHART J

PERCENT OF ADVANCEMENT PROGRAM EXPENDITURES FOR
FUND RAISING AND ALUMNI ACTIVITIES

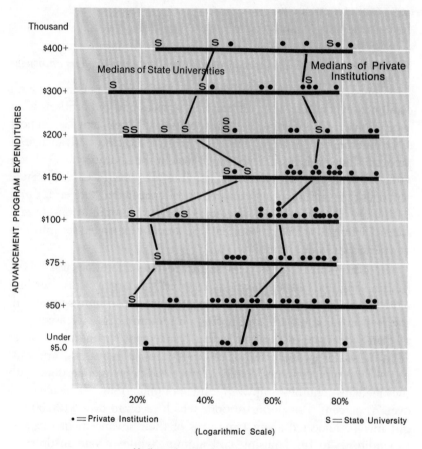

• = Private Institution   S = State University

(Logarithmic Scale)

Medians of private institutions and state universities
in each expenditure-size class are connected

personnel tend to have greater longevity at their particular institution —one college, for example, reported that their alumni executive had served 40 years. In many institutions, alumni activities began with the formation of an independent organization with a dues structure. Some of these persist, but they are a minority. Of the 94 institutions in the study sample which answered the question, only 12 (two private universities, three private coed colleges, and seven state universities) still had dues-paying alumni associations. The aura of "club" still surrounds much alumni activity. Yet all institutions realize that alumni are a basic source of gift dollars. Hence they all cultivate their alumni with various degrees of vigor.

One problem in comparing alumni-donated gift income among institutions is that no common definition of an "alumnus" exists. In some institutions, the student has to graduate; in others, one is called an alumnus after having attended one term or semester, or after having received an honorary degree. For the purposes of this study, "alumnus" was defined as any individual treated by his institution as an alumnus. For example, an institution may report 18,450 living alumni, but only 17,250 alumni "of record." That institution, by the study definition, has 17,250 alumni.

Another problem exists in making comparisons as to the alumni's effect on fund raising. At one time the alumni office handled all activities dealing with alumni, including fund raising. This has changed. In 40 percent of the institutions in the study sample, the alumni office did *no* fund raising. Chart K ranks by gift income both the institutions whose alumni office did no fund raising and those institutions in which alumni were solicited for gifts by the alumni office. The tendency is for the larger-gift income institutions to have the two activities separated. The reader will note that only five of 18 state universities and four of 12 private universities—although all 30 institutions have large alumni bodies—assigned fund raising among alumni to the alumni office. Furthermore, only two of the nine obtained any substantial dollar amounts of gifts from their alumni.

Alumni Gifts as Percent of Gift Income

Gifts from alumni are not a large percentage of gift income of the institutions studied, as Chart L indicates. The median for the sample

CHART K

FUND RAISING BY ALUMNI OFFICES

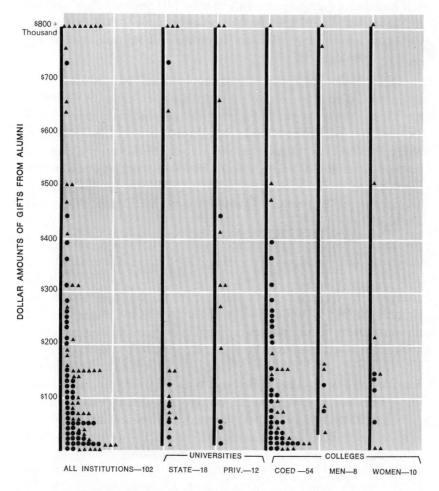

● = Institution Where Alumni Office Does Fund Raising From Alumni
▲ = Institution Where Alumni Office Does No Fund Raising From Alumni

was 16 percent. Private universities received nine percent of their gift income from alumni; state universities, 10 percent; and private colleges, 17 percent. Several interesting points can be noted from Chart L. First, as gifts from alumni increased, gifts from alumni as a percentage of gift income also increased. This could mean that the most successful fund raising institutions are successful because of their alumni, or that alumni are joining with other contributing individuals and organizations to achieve a successful fund raising program. Second, even with their larger numbers of alumni, state and private universities were generally below the median in terms of the importance of alumni gifts to the entire gift income program.

Third, just as advancement program expenditures per gift dollar decreased as gift income increased, cost per gift dollar from alumni decreased as alumni gift income increased. Alumni gifts from 14 institutions cost less than 10 cents per gift dollar to raise and, incidentally, in only one instance was the fund raising done by the alumni office. In seven institutions, the alumni operation cost more than it received in gifts, and in these institutions all but one office did its own fund raising. Fourth, the median cost per gift dollar from alumni for gift receipts under $20,000 was 90 cents. From $20,000 to $50,000 the median cost was 55 cents; and from $50,000 to $100,000 it was 38 cents. For gift totals of $100,000 the median dropped to about 20 cents. At $200,000 the median cost was down to 17 cents, and from $500,000 to $1 million and over it was seven cents.

Any alumni fund raising program can determine where it stands in relation to the above analysis by dividing gift dollars from alumni donors into alumni activities expenditures, and then comparing its cost per gift dollar with its gift income from alumni donors.

Alumni Office Staffs

Most institutions with fewer than 15,000 alumni of record had one professional staff person, excluding editors, in the alumni office; but of the institutions with 7,000 to 15,000 alumni, one out of every four had added a second professional person to the office. With institutions which have over 15,000 alumni of record, staffs which have three professionals begin to appear. Only five of the institutions in the study sample had professional alumni staffs of more than three people—of these, the largest was six.

CHART L

ALUMNI GIFTS AS A PERCENT OF GIFT INCOME

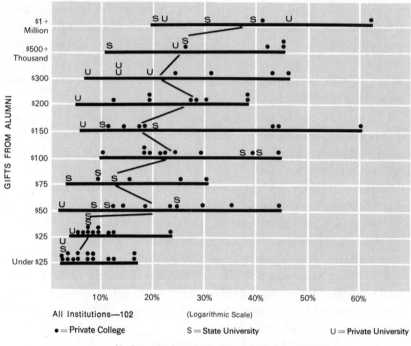

All Institutions—102   (Logarithmic Scale)

• = Private College   S = State University   U = Private University

Medians of private institutions and of state universities
in each expenditure-size class are connected

Cost per Alumnus

Although the figures may not be reliable because of imprecise definitions of alumnus and of expenditure composition, the median cost of maintaining or servicing an alumnus was $2.40 for alumni operations which did *no* fund raising and $3.20 for those which did. The range was from less than a dollar to more than $7.50. It was not possible to ascertain from the study data what each alumnus received for this expenditure, although the matter could be studied further in the future. Regardless of the cost, it is obvious that the addition of each alumnus adds a financial burden for the institution. With entering freshman classes of several thousand students, cost per alumnus becomes a significant factor.

The median of alumni who gave to their institutions for any purpose, including the alumni fund, was 18 percent. By type of institution, the medians were: state universities, 11 percent; private universities, 18 percent; private coed colleges, 17 percent; private men's colleges, 26 percent; and private women's colleges, 35 percent.

7. *Presidents, Trustees, and Staff in Fund Raising*

Fund raising activities cover an almost infinite range for a college or university. One of the most difficult activities to define, much less evaluate, is the solicitation of a gift. Figures obtained in the study are subject to all the individual interpretations of the respondents who answered the questionnaire. Perhaps some solicitation calls—especially those at the top level—can never be clearly identified. The questionnaire identified a solicitation call as a personal, face-to-face talk between a college or university representative and a prospective donor, in which a specific gift (not "your interest and support") was asked for openly and explicitly. Thus talks which are part of a group meeting are not included in this definition. The questionnaire sought to determine the number of solicitation calls made by president, trustees, and members of the institutional staff.

Presidents

Twenty-seven of the 31 state and private universities replied, but the answers were so varied that it was felt that more examples were needed for significant findings to be drawn from the data. However, with the private colleges there seemed to be some correlation between number of solicitation calls made by the president and amount of gifts. Of 74 such institutions in the sample, 63 replied. The data are shown in Table 6 below:

TABLE 6

Solicitation Calls by Private College Presidents

Number of President's Calls per Month	Institutions Above Median in Gifts For their Type of School				Institutions Below Median in Gifts For their Type of School			
	Coed	Men	Women	Total	Coed	Men	Women	Total
Over 10	14	1	1	16	7	—	—	7
5-9	7	2	1 ½	10 ½	9	1	1 ½	11 ½
1-4	3	1	1	5	6	1	1	8
No calls	—	—	—	—	2	2	1	5
				31 ½				31 ½

Note: The figure ½ refers to institutions directly at the median.

It will be noted that every president of an institution which was above the median in gift income made at least one solicitation call per month; five presidents of below median colleges made none. Since it is obvious that a president cannot—and should not—spend most of his time making gift solicitation calls, the optimum number of such calls is a matter of interest. Obviously it is dependent upon many factors. One call per month made on the "right" prospect can be more productive than 10 calls on less likely or able benefactors. However, certainly common sense and the study results would indicate that some degree of steady participation by the president in making solicitation calls will have a positive effect on the success of the institution's advancement program.

Trustees

Information on trustee activity in fund raising was obtained by the study questionnaire through asking about: (1) percent of trustees "active" and (2) number of actual solicitation calls made by an active trustee over an average 30-day period. The definition of an "active" trustee was left to the institution, i.e., if the institution termed a trustee active, he was considered to be so. The results are shown in the following table:

TABLE 7

Percent of "Active" Trustees

	Of the 105 Institutions
No reply	18%
No trustees active	13
Up to 10% trustees active	10
11 to 25% trustees active	15
26 to 50% trustees active	25
51 to 75% trustees active	12
76 to 100% trustees active	7
	100%

It is interesting to observe in considering these percentages that only 19 percent of the institutions in the sample termed more than 50 percent of their trustees "active." It is probably fair to assume that most of the respondents to the questionnaire were generous in their definition of "active." The point is, the situation may be worse than the figures indicate.

Relative to the second part of the question—solicitation calls by an "active" trustee—45 of the 76 which responded indicated one or two calls in an average month. Twenty-seven stated that their typically "active" trustees made *no* calls, and four said they made them only occasionally.

Staff Solicitation

Virtually no correlation was uncovered by the study between volume of gifts and frequency of staff solicitation not accompanied by the president or a volunteer (defined as an individual not employed by the institution, such as a trustee or alumnus). Of the 105 institutions in the study, 17 did not reply to these questions and 16 indicated no staff solicitations. The remaining 72 private colleges and state and private universities claimed a combined monthly average of more than 2,500 solicitation calls, or a monthly average of over 30 calls per institution. That, if true, is a good deal of solicitation, especially since it does not seem to correlate with level of gift income. Respondents indicated far fewer calls were made by staff accompanying the president or a trustee. About half of the institutions in the study sample reported faculty participation in gift solicitation, but here again no clear pattern of results emerged.

8. *Public Relations (Information Services and Publications) in the Advancement Program*

Some portion of today's public relations activities preceded the development of overall advancement programs on most campuses. Originally public relations at institutions of higher learning concentrated mainly on such activities as the issuance of news releases publicizing some event or aspect of the institution's educational endeavor. Today educational public relations encompasses a wide variety of activities designed to communicate and encourage understanding of the particular institution's programs and objectives. In addition to being a transmitter, the public relations officers must have receiver capabilities in order to do a better job of communicating and to function more effectively as a counselor to the president and chief administrative officers.

Organization of Public Relations

As mentioned previously, the study questionnaire tried to separate publications operations from other public relations activities because it is a substantial budget item on many campuses. It was found that private colleges—coed, men's, and women's—tended to group both information services and publications under one chief. Frequently there was no publications office as such, and publications were handled by the public relations office. Among both private and public universities there was roughly a 50-50 split in the handling of public relations and publications activities. Half of them had two separate departments, two chiefs, and budgets for each. In the other half, information services and publications were combined as was generally the case in the private colleges.

Activities

Several questions were asked concerning allocation of professional staff time of the personnel who work on public relations or information services and publications. Although the public relations concept has expanded greatly from its former news release orientation, a surprising finding was that the major single activity in nine of every 10 offices continued to be the preparation of news stories. The majority of the offices spent between 25 and 65 percent of their time preparing news releases, the median being about 45 percent. Only three offices allocated less than 25 percent of their time, and seven spent over 75 percent of their effort on news releases and stories.

Conversely, two out of three offices spent less than 10 percent of their energies on what was considered to be community relations. Two public relations offices indicated they allocated 50 percent of their time to community relations—a figure that was the highest found in the study. Two other offices spent 35 percent of their time on this important endeavor. A number of interesting questions could be raised from these findings—one of which is to wonder if the lack of attention shown by the public relations personnel was indicative of negligible interest in the community on the part of the entire institution. If so, this is puzzling, because universities and colleges are beginning to recognize more and more that they need to participate actively in community programs and politics. The participation must be as an interested community entity, and not for lobbying or "watchdog" purposes. Further research is necessary to shed light on these matters, especially since community relations is a nebulous term and good community relations does not start and stop in the public relations office.

The first question on the public relations portion of the questionnaire asked about the functions, broadly conceived, of the public relations office at the particular institution. The question was not devised to provide a statistical answer, but rather a qualitative answer. Its purpose was to determine whether institutional public relations offices have developed both long-range and intermediary objectives, and what their concept of public relations might be. Replies to this question defied quantitative analysis. They extended over the entire spectrum of such activities, from the specific to the general, from being responsible for putting on "X" event to spreading the good will of the institution. "Friend raising" was an activity mentioned a number of times.

In most cases, the presence of either long or short-range objectives was not alluded to by the respondents. Yet presumably short-range objectives, at least, exist. Perhaps public relations personnel do not systematically analyze activities from this perspective. It would be reasonable to assume from responses to the questionnaire that identification of specific long and short-range objectives, along with the systematic planning of methods of implementation, are lacking in the public relations offices of most universities and colleges. In other words, the degree of success of a public relations office may depend excessively on intuition and native ability, rather than upon systematic planning.

Mailing Lists

Excluding news media, six broad categories of potential receivers of institutional mailings—alumni, present and prospective students, parents, faculty, donors, and prospects—were considered. It was assumed that trustees, legislators, and other key individuals would be handled specially. Institutions attempted to divide their mailings into two general categories of purpose: public relations and fund raising. The results of the study were:

TABLE 8

Distribution of Public Relations and Fund Raising Mailings to Certain Groups

Group Receiving Mailings	Percent of Institutions Sending Public Relations Mailings	Percent of Institutions Sending Fund Raising Mailings
Alumni	98%	95%
Students	60	13
Faculty	92	36
Donors	78	79
Prospects	69	73
Parents	83	63

The question of who and how many other groups and individuals, in addition to alumni, should be kept on the mailing list is a knotty one.

CHART M

Copy Preparation by Information Services or Publications Office

Type of Publication(s)	Private Colleges		Private Universities		State Universities		All	
Catalog	27 of 67 or	40%	4 of 12 or	33%	9 of 17 or	53%	40 of 96 or	42%
Annual Report	25 of 56	43	6 of 12	50	11 of 15	73	42 of 83	51
Admissions	42 of 67	63	7 of 12	58	11 of 17	65	60 of 96	63
Alumni Magazine	37 of 66	66	7 of 12	58	2 of 17	12	46 of 95	48
University Magazine	21 of 24	88	7 of 7	100	8 of 8	100	36 of 39	92
Fund Raising Publications	24 of 67	36	7 of 12	58	3 of 17	18	34 of 96	35
Publications for Students	3 of 65	5	1 of 12	8	2 of 17	12	6 of 94	6
News Bulletin for Faculty	32 of 52	62	10 of 12	83	14 of 17	82	56 of 81	69

* Out of the 105 institutions in the study sample, 96 institutions reported.

No correlation was found in this study between size of list, and size of institution or percentage of non-alumni to alumni. Some private institutions with large non-alumni mailing lists had small gift dollar incomes, while others with relatively small lists had large gift dollar receipts.

Publications

Of all the activities examined in the study, publications showed the least uniformity of practice. There was an extremely wide variety of publications, and an equally wide variety of offices producing them. For purposes of the analysis, eight common and important types of publications were considered from the standpoints of copy preparation and the extent to which information services or publications offices are involved, either alone or in cooperation with other offices. Chart M displays the findings.

9. Summary of Study Findings

Various possible yardsticks for measuring effectiveness of advancement programs in universities and colleges were examined in the analysis of study data. Some of the factors considered in this preliminary and exploratory study were: gift income, gifts as a percentage of educational and general expenditures, advancement program expenditures as percentages of gift income and of educational and general expenditures, cost of gifts, relation between gifts and fund raising and public relations budgets, number of gift solicitation calls, and alumni office activities and alumni gifts. Also considered were such factors as the organization of advancement programs, and staff sizes and salaries. Some other possible yardsticks and factors which were examined, but not found relevant, were: type of institution, enrollment, expenditures per student, and endowment per student, to mention a few.

Gift income exclusive of deferred gifts was found to be a useful and relatively undistorted yardstick. An observation made after examining the data was that institutions which fall into similar gift income ranges were found to be similar in many ways such as in advancement program expenditures, staff sizes, and complexity of advancement program. These similarities tended to hold regardless of differences in type of institution or enrollment. The study's findings about the present status of college advancement programs suggest a number of ways of strengthening their performance and enhancing institutional understanding and support. Indicators and yardsticks of performance need to be established and tested over a period of years to determine their validity. Data collection systems must be expanded and improved to provide reliable information. Even with valid indicators and reliable information, the art and science of sound management are still necessary for an institution to achieve maximum productivity from its advancement programs. These major opportunities, and others to which attention should be addressed, are dealt with in the chapters which follow.

CHAPTER III

Organizing the Advancement Program

The second chapter presented an analysis of the study's findings about the present status of university and college advancement programs. Chapters III and IV will attempt to project the quantitative analysis into guidelines for the organizing, planning and evaluating of an institutional advancement program.

A. WHY AN ORGANIZATION?

Good organizational structure and good organization are not things which simply develop themselves, or exist in a vacuum, or are ends in themselves. Their importance is that they provide a way of approaching and accomplishing a given task or responsibility in an orderly, systematic manner. An organized approach facilitates the identification of objectives, the planning of programs and policies, the allocation of human and financial resources, and the establishment of control over operations. The central focus of this chapter is on the organization of advancement programs. The suggestions given are based on the analysis of the study data, campus interviews, and management experience of consultants and practitioners.

The advancement program—the overall program whose purpose is to advance the understanding and support of the particular institution —is an integral part of any college or university. The manager of this program needs immediate access to the president of the institution, and, likewise, the president must have close control of the program in order for it to be coordinated with all academic, student and business affairs. Furthermore, if the institution is to derive maximum effectiveness from its advancement program, the manager must be a part of the president's chief executive staff together with managers of the academic, student, and business activities. Only in this manner can the president coordinate and direct effectively the entire operation of the institution.

Evidence obtained from the study analysis and from interviews and consultations indicates that the centralized approach—the alignment of all advancement program activities under one manager—is an organizational trend in higher education. In addition, program or project planning is increasingly being implemented, probably getting its greatest boost from the numerous capital fund raising campaigns.

The advantages of a centralized approach and program planning can be summarized as follows:

... centralizes accountability and responsibility under the president;

... encourages systematic planning, implementation and evaluation;

... expedites communication;

... provides more coordination and greater flexibility, thereby avoiding some of the causes of duplication and inefficiency.

It should be noted that each member of the president's chief executive staff—which has various names in individual institutions—is a manager regardless of title because he is charged with the planning, implementation, and evaluation of the substantial activities within his area of responsibility. Likewise, each must work with the others under the direction of the president toward planning, implementing, and evaluating the institution's total educational program. Since each manager should be held accountable for his area of responsibility, he must be involved in the planning process at the time that objectives and methods of implementation are established. The planning and evaluation of an advancement program will be discussed in greater detail in the following pages, with an elaboration of these basic points.

B. The Advancement Program Manager and His Relations with the Institution's Governing Structure

1. *Relationship with the President*

The president, as chief executive officer, must maintain a close professional relationship with the manager of the advancement program, since the two will find themselves working with many of the same people, for example, governing board members, influential businessmen, alumni, government leaders, and persons from other educational institutions.

Therefore, the president should select a highly motivated, performance oriented, advancement program manager whom he respects and in whom he has complete confidence. It is important that this individual's personal traits be such that the president can work with him compatibly. The individual must be qualified in terms of experience and performance, otherwise the responsibilities and demands are unfair to him and the institution. The president should make it a rule not to bypass his manager in matters of policy consideration or implementation; nor should the manager expect the president never to talk or work with any of the manager's subordinates.

2. *Relationship with the Governing Board*

A parallel situation exists with respect to the close relationship that should be maintained between the manager of the advancement program and the governing board of the institution. The relationships between members of the institution's governing board and the advancement program manager and his staff members are crucial. The board retains the president and through him the governing policies established by the board are carried out.

The manager of the advancement program and some members of his staff will need to work closely with the governing board as they assist the president in accomplishing financial support objectives. Care must be taken that this working relationship is always within previously established policy and that each person respects the other's area of responsibility. A president will not help himself by jealously guarding his access to members of the governing board. At the same time, neither board members nor the manager should take advantage of their working relationship to bypass presidential directives or second-guess his decisions. Personal discipline and integrity are vital to the effectiveness of the working relationship and the maintenance of confidence, good morale, and good communication.

C. Qualities and Characteristics of the Advancement Program Manager

No less care should be taken in the selection of a manager of the advancement program than in the picking of any other executive officer. Job descriptions will vary at different institutions, but the following checklist describes generally the role of the manager of an institution's advancement program, and suggests some of the qualities needed.

The manager will have to:

... work closely with and command the respect of the president, the other executive officers, and the governing board;

... work closely with and gain the respect of faculty members;

... participate in institutional planning and decision-making;

... have the executive ability to assign responsibility and establish priorities for a multitude of activities;

... be familiar enough with the techniques of fund raising, public relations, and alumni programs to plan, coordinate, and evaluate these activities;

... serve as one of the institution's principal emissaries with various influential individuals and groups;

... articulate the institution's programs and objectives in a convincing and persuasive manner;

... know business procedures in order to establish and maintain an efficient, effective organization;

.... constantly seek more creative, imaginative ways to further the understanding and support of the institution.

The manager of the advancement program must be thoroughly conversant with the academic program and educational goals, student selection, student life, business affairs, physical plant planning, and all other aspects of the institution. Only through this total perspective of his institution, together with a thorough grounding in the practices of higher education on the national scene, can the manager plan and implement successfully a program designed to increase the understanding and support of his particular institution.

The manager of the advancement program must also combine the ingenuity and far-sighted talents of innovator, planner, and researcher with the pragmatic qualities of a business executive. He will have to be conversant with the philosophies and practices of both the academician and businessman because he is the bridge between them. He must know how research in social psychology, management psychology, group dynamics, and effective techniques of communication and persuasion will help him in organizing, planning, and evaluating the advancement program.

It should be obvious that a versatile and highly competent generalist—not a specialist—is required. It is for this reason that the person selected for the manager's position should have had a variety of assignments and responsibilities which would equip him for the broad range of duties.

It is not imperative, however, for the manager to have moved up through the ranks of an institution's public relations, development, or alumni offices; but practical experience in these areas would certainly provide him with perspective and probably make his subordinates' acceptance of his directives easier. Neither is it imperative for the manager to have had educational experience, but the president should be convinced that he can gain familiarity and sympathy with this area, and that his other experience more than offsets this deficiency. What is especially important to the president is that the person whom he selects has demonstrated successful administrative performance in some type of position in which he was required to meet certain specified standards. The qualifications of the advancement program manager must include evidence of proven performance and the willingness to assume personal responsibility for a program.

D. Need for Institutional Training Programs

A great shortage of trained executive personnel exists today in higher education. Universities and colleges have generally not planned for their administrative needs as much as they have for faculty requirements. This often means the larger or more established institutions will be able to exercise greater selectivity in obtaining advancement program personnel than most of their smaller or less well known neighbors. At present only a few institutions provide any degree of formalized administrative training programs, and administrative internships are just being initiated on a modest basis in higher education. However, in the long run, institutions of all sizes will find they must have more formalized training programs to keep pace with personnel requirements in administrative areas.

A president seeking to staff key executive positions, such as the manager of the advancement program, must live with today's shortage and learn to work within its limits. Yet, at the same time, he should be developing administrative training procedures at his own institution and promoting similar programs throughout higher education. Planning for a continuing supply of competent managerial leadership is as important to the future vitality of an institution as academic, financial, and physical plant planning.

It can be expected that increasingly institutions will see the need for establishing their own administrative training programs. The extent of the program will depend upon the size of the institution and its personnel requirements. However, formalized training programs can be implemented just as easily and can be just as effective at small colleges as at large universities. Training programs will probably be designed for promising young people entering the administrative ranks and should take into consideration the need for exposure to all activities of the institution. The broader his perspective, the better the trainee will perform in his specific assignment.

In addition, the training program should be designed to provide opportunities for, and even encourage, persons to move among offices within the advancement program area, as well as within other administrative departments of the institution. A reasonable degree of free flow of personnel among all administrative offices enhances career opportunities within the institution and provides a promising executive with the all-important breadth of experience. Too often a person's career progression is vertical—for example, teacher . . . department head . . . dean; or staff associate . . . director of development . . . vice president. Horizontal progression is valuable too. At present little opportunity is afforded for broadening horizons and thereby gaining empathy and varied experience—two key factors in enlightened leadership.

Only through well-designed administrative training programs will education be able to increase the competency of its executive personnel and overcome the shortage of experienced administrative persons, especially in the institutional advancement area. A president of a university or college should examine what he is doing to help solve this problem.

E. CHECKLIST FOR THE ORGANIZATION OF THE ADVANCEMENT PROGRAM

Certain principles for organizing the advancement program can be applied regardless of the size or type of institution. But specifics, in terms of numbers of people and particular job descriptions, will vary according to the extent and complexity of the program.

Organization means both a concept and a structure to accomplish stated goals. The concept of organization pertains to good management policies, whereas the structure manifests itself in lines of staff authority and specific operational procedures. Sound principles of management can be more effectively applied in a well-designed organization—one that is not static and one that is subject to constant review to determine how it can be improved. The organizational chart is not an exercise in drawing diagrams, but is properly an accurate visual portrayal of the procedures deemed necessary to obtain the desired objectives. The organizational chart serves both executive and staff in showing authority, functions, and lines of communication.

Few presidents are given the opportunity of organizing and staffing an advancement program from scratch. Nevertheless, chief executives faced with the realities of an existing structure and personnel can still evaluate them in terms of their potential and actual performance in achieving appropriate goals. An advancement program's organizational plan should:

    ... establish authority and responsibility;

    ... place the entire coordinated group of activities immediately under the president;

    ... enable the president to centralize responsibility and accountability;

... encourage and provide a mechanism for coordinated planning, implementation, and evaluation of all activities, such as financial support, information services, and publication programs;

... provide for free flow of two-way communication;

... insure flexibility and the implementation of structural and procedural changes as necessary.

Some of the guidelines overlap in part, but the key considerations in any organizational plan are planning, responsibility, and evaluation. Sound organizational procedures will go far to eliminate ineffective, inefficient programs, uncontrolled activities, and internal personnel conflicts caused by overlapping or fuzzy areas of authority.

Tradition and existing personnel are probably the two greatest compromising forces exerted on sound principles of organization. Historical precedent, while an important consideration, should not prohibit the development of new or modified approaches to solving problems. In fact, there is no other real choice, for the college or university president today is faced with the realities that:

... subject matter and teaching methods have changed drastically;

... persons desire higher education to meet many different, as well as many new, objectives;

... American social and political life is altering;

... wealth and economic power are to some extent moving into different hands.

These are just a few changes which affect and will continue to affect higher education. Many other examples could be mentioned, but these serve to illustrate the point. It is only reasonable to assume that the organizational plan of the entire university, and particularly that of the advancement program, must undergo periodic analysis and alteration.

Traditions die quickly without people who have a vested interest to perpetuate them. The traditions which should be preserved are those which demand a high quality of accomplishment, a constant search for improved performance, and a professional approach toward increasing the understanding and support of higher education. It is up to each institution to define these concepts operationally in terms of its own purposes. But traditional events, organizations, and procedures which no longer meet a critical, unbiased verdict as to their appropriateness and utility are not worthy of perpetuation. Beyond the ability to conduct critical, unbiased evaluations, presidents and managers of the advancement program need the courage to implement their findings.

F. The Centralized Organizational Approach

The trend in the organization of advancement programs, as pointed out in the previous chapter, is toward the centralized approach. This approach is defined as the organizational structure in which all activities related to the advancement program are grouped together under a single coordinating manager who, with his staff, has the responsibility of seeing that the components of the program are administered effectively and that the total job is done. Generally speaking, it has been found that the centralized approach is the most effective way to provide the necessary leadership for the advancement program.

An important point should be noted before beginning any discussion of either organizational structures or of charts illustrating them. People, as well as structure, are key factors in making any organization work, and no amount of manipulation of diagrams can provide that magic ingredient. On the other hand, unsound or unclear organizational procedures can be a source of inefficiency and ineffectiveness, and sometimes the study of organizational charts can help to point up where the problem exists.

Chart N represents an analysis of organizational requirements along the lines of activities or functions, without regard for the constituencies served by each individual activity. In the diagram, boxes are used only for the president and manager of the advancement program, because no attempt is made here to indicate the numbers of individuals who should be assigned to all or parts of the six broad advancement program functions. It is imperative that the program be "consumer-oriented"—in other words, established with the unique characteristics of its particular constituencies in mind. Each constituency will be served to varying degrees by all six of the functions, but the number of staff members involved directly with any one of the institution's constituencies, and the number of constituencies to be served by any one person, are management decisions.

	FUNCTION	CONSTITUENCY
Institutional Planning ↓ President Advancement Program Manager	**Financial Support:** Implementation of solicitation programs appropriate to each constituency, Government liaison **Information Services:** News Releases, Media servicing, Film-TV script preparation and production coordination **Publication Services:** Copy preparation, layout and design coordination of all magazines, brochures, folders, etc., for all the institution's departments and constituencies **Special Events:** Dedications, Commencements, Convocations, Homecomings and reunions, Anniversaries, Major off-campus programs **Research and Evaluation:** Institutional and constituency research for use in planning and evaluating results of various advancement program projects **General Administrative Services:** Secretarial and support staff, Printing and duplicating, Records (including fund raising), Personnel, Photo laboratory	Alumni Business and Industry Communications Media Faculty and Staff Foundations Governing Board Governments { Local State Federal Other Individuals, Donors, Opinion Leaders, Prospects Parents Religious Denominations Students

Regardless of the size or type of institution, the advancement program manager should find that most of the activities falling within his purview are classified under one of Chart N's six broad headings: financial support, information services, publications services, special events, research and evaluation, and general administrative services. Activities such as student recruitment and management of the university press are part of the advancement program on some campuses, but they are most generally placed in the academic area.

The six broad functional areas comprising institutional advancement programs are described below in greater detail. Although the total advancement organization directs its attention to all constituencies, nevertheless each professional staff member will have his particular activities to perform with one or more constituencies kept specially in mind.

Financial Support Function—consists of such activities as fact-finding about prospects and solicitation of gifts from individuals and groups within the institution's constituencies, as well as appropriate liaison with fund-granting agencies of local, state and federal governments.

Information Services Function—consists of such activities as preparation and dissemination of news and other information on the institution's programs, objectives, and policies, servicing of requests from news media, and preparation of scripts and coordination of the production of promotional or informative films and TV clips issued by the institution.

Publications Services Function—consists of such activities as preparation and editing of copy, and coordination of layout and design of magazines, brochures, folders, and other items for all the institution's departments and constituencies.

Special Events Function—consists of administration of principal special events such as dedications, commencements, convocations, homecomings, reunions, anniversaries, and major off-campus programs, with the degree of involvement dependent upon many factors.

Research and Evaluation Function—consists of such activities as direction of research projects designed to determine constituent attitudes, evaluation of specific projects, evaluation of the performance of the advancement program, and related activities according to established objectives and goals.

General Administrative Services Function—consists of activities such as the direction and coordination of programs, offices, and persons in supportive roles, for example, secretarial staff, printing and duplicating department, records department (including gift records), photo laboratory, and personnel records and recruitment (if not handled centrally in the institution).

Constituencies which are commonly relevant to institutions of higher learning are: alumni, business and industry, communications media, faculty and administrative and research staff, foundations, governments (local, state, federal), other individuals (donors, opinion leaders, prospects), parents, religious denominations, students, and governing board members. Many persons fall under more than one category. The constituencies listed in the far right-hand column of Chart N are by no means inclusive, but represent the vast majority of groups with whom the average institution of higher education will work. Broad constituencies are listed for convenience, but ultimately smaller sub-groups and individuals are the important consideration. One of the great pitfalls of educational public relations and development programs is the tendency to think in terms of group labels such as corporate executives, alumni, and parents. One individual may play many roles even with respect to the same institution. For example, he may be a parent, and also an alumnus, businessman, trustee, and community resident. In addition, all members of a group do not respond in the same way. People think as individuals and do not react as "the alumni," "the business world," or "parents."

The more an advancement program manager analyzes his constituencies the more he will recognize that all six major advancement program functions are relevant to each constituency, but in differing degrees. For example, most constituencies are served by information, publications, and special events activities, which in many cases are followed by appeals for financial support. Also relevant to every advancement program activity are general administrative services, and research and evaluation, which are essential for effective planning of the entire advancement program.

The number of staff members serving any one of the broad functions, or the number of activities handled by one person, will depend upon the decisions of the manager of the advancement program. The study found the amount of resources and number of personnel committed to an advancement program is unrelated to enrollment or complexity of the educational program of the institution. Many four-year liberal arts colleges have larger and more sophisticated advancement programs than large universities.

When planning the organizational structure of the advancement program and the job descriptions of the various individuals, the manager should consider functions first, constituencies second. For example, the size of the publications department should be governed by the variety of publications. The same is true of information and publications services, where writers can certainly prepare copy for fund raising projects or alumni activities as well as for news releases and magazines. In some situations, double utilization of personnel may be very effective. While training or experience may be a problem at the outset, these can be acquired. By this means personnel utilization can become more efficient, and the advancement program manager gains more flexibility.

Maximum personnel utilization is important to advancement program staffs of all sizes. The larger a staff, the greater the number of persons likely to be assigned to narrow areas of responsibility, such as the director of corporate solicitation, or the director of the annual fund. But the more limited a person's responsibilities, the more danger there is that he will become extremely narrow and act to retard progress and improvement of the advancement program.

By first considering function, the manager will be better able to conduct program and project planning so as to reap the advantages of personnel and budget conservation. Special programs to cope with an episode of student disruption, or to stage a special fund raising campaign, or to prepare for an inauguration can often be handled with existing personnel selected from several departments and working under a project director.

No attempt has been made in Chart N to suggest titles or departmental alignment. Organizational boxes are not used because these tend to be automatically translated into people, and the number of persons and individual job descriptions within an advancement program has to be determined by the particular manager. The number of professionals is importantly related to the objectives and complexity of the advancement program, and not simply to factors such as the type of institution, its enrollment, living alumni, and location.

However, by considering the activities relating to the six broad functions, one can sketch out a brief job description of each of the persons who might occupy these slots. Probably the least commonly employed of the functions is that of research and evaluation, but properly administered it could be one of the most valuable to the manager. Another function, less common than the others, is that of special events, although it is becoming increasingly popular to designate a person to serve as college or university marshal or director of special programs and projects, with the task of coordinating them. Yet many smaller advancement programs do not have this need and could combine functions. If each of the six functions were to be translated into positions, managers of large advancement programs might prefer for general administrative services to report to one of the other executives or to an administrative assistant. On smaller staffs, this function probably would be administered by a competent secretary.

G. Translating Functions into Positions

The great difficulty in providing relevant organizational guidelines for an institution's advancement program is that no two institutions are exactly the same. Size, goals, sources of financial support, and other factors can differ considerably. Thus it cannot be expected that an organizational chart from one institution could apply to another without any modifications. But a chart can prove helpful in suggesting various organizational solutions which, with careful analysis, can perhaps be tailored into an effective organizational structure appropriate to the institution's advancement program goals. As part of the prerequisite analysis, institutional goals, sources of support, financial potential, and available resources must be scrutinized thoroughly.

Chart N provides a description of the functions common to most —if not all—advancement programs. But it is obvious that institutions would not divide their resources in staff and money equally among the six broad functional categories. The desired optimal allocation to each function is a difficult subject upon which to generalize. However, in Chart O an attempt is made to provide a guideline for one possible approach to the allocation of professional personnel with staffs of various sizes. Viewed another way, the chart also provides guidelines for staff assignments as an advancement program expands—say, from four persons to six, or from eight persons to 10 or 12—to meet increased requirements. Of course, the chart is only a guide and must be adapted by institutions studying it.

Several presuppositions are incorporated in Chart O:

First, four persons—maybe three in certain cases—constitute the minimum professional staff for an effective advancement program; otherwise the staff will be spread so thin that effective impact would be jeopardized.

Second, financial support is the objective of all advancement programs, regardless of whether the institution is public or private, and, therefore, the largest proportion of the professional staff should be assigned to this function.

Third, specific job descriptions and constituency assignments within the six broad functions must not omit consideration of the unique characteristics and needs of the specific institution. For example, one institution with eight professional staff members may have two persons assigned to alumni relations and fund raising, while another institution with comparable professional staff may decide, because of its immediate needs, to place only one person in alumni work and assign another person to concentrate on corporate fund raising.

Fourth, competent administrative and secretarial staff can supplement, or in some cases substitute for, professionals in carrying out some of a function's activities.

In Chart O, the asterisks represent the original four professional staff members (first presupposition). One person, either the staffer who handles information services, or the financial support function (whichever one is *not* also manager of the advancement program) would also handle special events. It is entirely possible—and not undesirable—that each of the four would handle his own specific special events.

The allocation of duties, or job descriptions, of additions to the original four professional staff persons are indicated by letters from A to H in sequence of their addition. For instance, with the first addition,

CHART O

Each asterisk represents one of the original four professional staff members.

(Letters designate the sequential progression of staff expansion, i.e., A and B are added as staff expands from four to six, C and D from six to eight, etc.).

Advancement Program Functions [1]

Staff Size	Information Services	Publication Services	Special Events	Financial Support	Research and Evaluation	Administrative Services
4	*[3]	*	*[2]	*[3] *		
6	*	*	A	* A B	B	
8	* D	* D	A	* * B C	B	D
10	* D	* D	A	* * B C F	B	E
12	* D	* G	A	* * C F H	B	E

Notes (1) Functions are not titles, but activities performed by professional staff regardless of title. A good example is the alumni relations director who probably performs some part of all six functions in serving his constituency.

(2) Special events would be the responsibility of either the chief person in information services or financial support (whichever one was not also manager of the advancement program).

(3) One of these two persons would be the manager of the advancement program, in addition to functioning in the information services or financial support area.

"A", special events would receive direct coordination and financial support would get additional assistance. When bringing a sixth person into the advancement program is contemplated, consideration should be given to supervision of research and evaluation activities in addition to further emphasis in financial support activities. The chart does not intend to indicate that the fifth person handles special events or that the sixth staffer becomes charged with research and evaluation. It (the chart) merely indicates a suggested allocation of total professional staff time available. The vertical columns are functions, or activities, not people or titles.

Through job descriptions and as-best-possible analysis of time expended, the manager can regulate the allocation of his staff resources. He is the best person to judge the allocation of six professionals—or even eight or 10—toward accomplishing the objectives of the advancement program.

Chart O can also serve as the format for a complete analysis of personnel allocation. Disregarding the asterisks and letters which denote original staff and additions in sequence, the chart looks like this for full-time equivalent allocation of personnel:

CHART P

Allocation of Personnel

Staff Size	Information Services	Publications Services	Special Events	Financial Support	Research Evaluation	Administrative Services
4	¾	1	¼	2		
6	1	1	½	3	½	
8	1 ¼	1 ¼	1	3 ¾	½	¼
10	1 ¼	1 ½	1	4 ¼	1	1
12	2	2	1	5	1	1

Note: Each person's time is allocated in quarters among each of the six function areas. One full-time equivalent (FTE) person might actually be two people spending approximately one-half time performing the function, or it might be two people, one spending three-quarters time and the other one-quarter. Any combination of people and FTE is possible and a break down of fifths or thirds might be more desirable than quarters.

The value of Chart P to the manager of the advancement program is to provide a guide to the technique of personnel resources allocation. Allocation as presented in the chart can certainly be debated relative to any given institutional situation. Factors such as institutional goals, personnel strengths, historical characteristics, and established patterns of support can alter the allocation pattern.

Regardless of his present situation and allocation of personnel, a manager needs to determine this allocation and maintain it under constant review relative to his objectives. It will not be a simple matter to determine the amount of time a staff member divides among the six function areas. Few professional staffers devote all their energies exclusively to any one of the areas. In the beginning rough approximation is all that will be possible, but experience and observation should help refine these estimates. Constant analysis of one's work is an excellent discipline and one of the secrets to greater effectiveness and efficiency.

H. ALTERNATE ORGANIZATIONAL PATTERNS

A large number of institutions have affiliated with them semi-autonomous bodies, and yet many of these arrangements appear to be effective and efficient. Some of these are the result of tradition or personnel considerations, while others are brought about by legal requirements.

1. *Development "Foundations"*

The fund raising "foundation" is an example of an alternate organizational pattern. In some institutions, the alumni years ago organized a foundation to solicit funds for particular purposes, while in other institutions, the term "foundation" was selected as a convenient label for the group of individuals organized by the institution to solicit money. In still other institutions, state regulations forbade or made it difficult for state institutions to receive private gifts, and this situation in turn led to the establishment of privately incorporated "foundations" to solicit and disburse private gift dollars.

Regardless of origin, the fund raising or development foundation is a matter of organizational concern for the president and advancement program manager. If the foundation exists in name only, the chief concern is probably the avoidance of confusion on the part of the donor. If, on the other hand, a separately established governing board is involved, the president and manager of the advancement program may be saddled with a major organizational problem. In such a case, the two named individuals have two alternatives: either to attempt to change the charter or regulation which dictates the separate status or to manage by persuasion.

Any organization established to solicit funds in the name of a particular institution should have a majority of the executive leadership of that institution on its governing board. In other words, the XYZ University Foundation board of governors should be composed of the president and chairman of the board of XYZ University together with enough XYZ University personnel to insure, if they vote together, that solicitation of funds will not be for purposes contrary to the institution's policies, and that the allocation of gift income will be in accordance with important needs and goals.

If state law presently prohibits a state institution of higher learning from receiving private gift dollars directly, and currently no acceptable arrangement exists for receiving these contributions, every effort should be made to change that law. Barring successful action to change the law, the institution should definitely establish an independently incorporated fund raising foundation even if there is risk of creating some organizational problems. Fortunately, many independent development foundations work within the existing organizational pattern of the institution. In fact, in many cases professional staff personnel hold dual appointments, officially serving both the institution and the foundation. Management is not a problem in these instances as it would be for development foundations which work entirely outside the existing organization.

2. *Alumni Associations*

The independent alumni association can also present an organizational problem, although the alumni association which is truly independent—legally and financially—is a rarity. Only a handful are still in existence. However, most alumni associations, legally independent or not, have their own governing boards.

Close cooperation is the key if both the institution and the alumni association are to fulfill sucessfully their respective objectives. If it is truly advantageous for the alumni association to maintain completely separate legal identity, good communication must be maintained and all phases of the planning, implementing, and evaluating of activities should be handled in close concert with the manager of the advancement program. Otherwise, duplication and missed opportunities can result.

Resources committed by the institution to the advancement of its alumni's understanding and support should generally be in accord with the current and near-future potential of the alumni. Large sums of money have been expended on projects whose chief justification was some vaguely defined anticipation of support in the future. Fund raising projects designed to have long-range future outcomes, such as deferred giving programs, are to be strongly encouraged; but as with deferred gifts, there should be some reasonably documentable expectation of return on the institution's investment of time and money.

Any constituency-oriented professional staff, such as those employed by alumni associations, faces the danger of becoming isolated from the mainstream of institutional planning. Also, as mentioned earlier, the potential pitfalls of group opinions—"the alumni think . . ." —are present in constituency-oriented staffs. Effective communication and coordinated planning pursued along functional lines can help overcome these dangers.

CHAPTER IV

Planning and Evaluating the Advancement Program

A. The Planning Process

Not so many years ago, it was thought that the mounting of a fund raising campaign and an organization to carry on the related mechanics were all that were necessary in raising outside financial support. Some presidents selected and approved (and, unfortunately, some still do) a dollar figure for a fund raising effort without having developed data to show why the established goal was "X" dollars rather than some other figure. Experience has shown, however, that launching fund raising campaigns which are not supported by sound plans and effective management may jeopardize their success. Since sound planning is a prerequisite both for sound implementation of programs and for meaningful evaluation, a brief discussion of the planning process is presented prior to discussion of the evaluation process.

1. *What is Planning?*

Planning involves charting a course which will take an educational institution from the present to the future over some stated period of time. Sophisticated planners seek to develop a long-range 10 to 15-year plan, together with short-range plans to achieve each step along the way. These plans are re-examined and adjusted every two or three years. Both long and short-range plans can be made only after clear-cut establishment of a number of educational goals and policies, as well as analysis of basic data pertaining to such matters as economic projec-

72

tions, curriculum changes, educational plant usage, academic facility requirements, resident and graduate enrollment needs, instructional costs, and availability of financing.

In the construction of a plan, the institution's objectives must be reviewed in order to adjust them realistically to fit anticipated resources and educational programs. For example, size, both overall and by components, must be determined on the basis of educational objectives and financial requirements and resources; the physical facilities and manpower required to attain objectives must be identified; and, finally, the capital and operating costs required to implement these plans must be calculated. The ways in which plans are to be implemented should be expressed each year in annual operating budgets. The annual budget translates into financial terms the institution's goals, together with the physical and human requirements for achieving those goals.

2. Organizing the Planning Process

Many colleges and universities have been slow in giving organizational recognition to the need for an effective planning function. Some presidents assume personal responsibility for planning, thus revealing considerable managerial naïveté. The detailed analysis involved in the kind of planning just described is more than can possibly be done by a person who is busy with many other responsibilities.

Alternatively, the planning function is often apportioned by assigning responsibility for educational or academic planning to the chief academic officer below the president, financial planning to the financial officer, and physical planning to still another administrator, with each officer responsible for planning for his respective area. The resulting outlines of objectives, plans, and necessary expenditures are presented to the governing board by the president; the board reviews and approves the plans, and authorizes the president and the administration to prepare plans in detail. Responsibilities for various portions of the overall plan are then discharged by the administrative officers (under the president) who originally drafted the plans. The missing link in this approach is the existence of an officer with specific responsibility for seeing that planning is done and for coordinating the plans on behalf of the president.

In recognition of this need, and as a third approach, in some colleges and universities the responsibility both for planning in his own area and for coordinating overall plans is given to the chief academic administrative officer—often the provost or vice president for academic affairs—who then collaborates with other administrative officers at this level to formulate detailed plans. This assignment is made in view of the centrality of educational policies and programs, and assumes that all plans should be coordinated around the institution's educational mission. Other institutions assign the responsibility to a vice president of finance. Still others may have a director or a coordinator of planning, who reports as a staff officer to the president and works with the various vice presidents in developing plans.

Whatever the arrangement, it is chiefly important to recognize the need for assigning one individual to take responsibility for long-range planning and coordination, and for the implementing of crucial and relevant sequential activities. Next in importance is making organizational provision for this function, by clearly designating someone in the top administrative structure to see that proper staff support is provided for planning, and that the necessary factual data are developed and analyzed in order to support and give substance to elements to be considered in decision-making.

Some development officers have argued that their fund raising office is the logical spot to coordinate all planning. For a variety of reasons, however, presidents have frequently been reluctant to assign the responsibility to that office. Faculties might feel the educational program would be tailored to financial expediencies; the particular officer might lack sufficient capacity for dealing with academic, physical plant, and financial problems and forecasts; and the various advancement program activities are not usually involved in the substantive aspects of planning to the same extent as are the academic, business, and financial offices.

The president should first determine where the greatest capabilities and strengths for planning reside, and then place responsibility there. As a practical matter, there are sound reasons why the chief advancement program manager should not, as a matter of principle, also seek to be recognized as the chief planning officer. Some possible reasons against it are that: the manager is probably very busy with his own activities; he is less involved with the academic area than are some of the other administrators; he may tend to view planning too much from the financial support point of view. If, as a vice president, however, the advancement program manager is clearly regarded as having great competence in planning, and if this talent is recognized, accepted, and respected, then there may be excellent reasons for lodging this responsibility with him.

The president should apply as rigorous requirements to the chief academic and business officers as he does to other personnel in determining where to place central responsibility for planning. Many chief academic and business officers are no more qualified than are many managers of advancement programs. Even if a member of the executive staff is qualified and available, the president will still want to consider hiring an individual to be the planning officer.

3. *An Organizational Structure for the Planning Process*

Each of the institution's four principal executive officers—academic, student affairs, business, and advancement—has enough to do in implementing, planning and evaluating the activities immediately under his own jurisdiction, so that total institutional planning, if it is assigned to any of them, might get far less attention than it deserves. For this reason, an organizational procedure along the following lines is suggested:

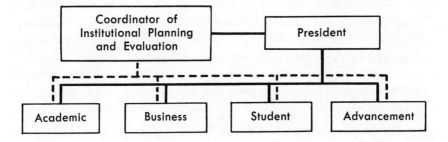

Using this organizational plan, an institution would have the planning officer report directly to the president in a staff role. In turn, the office would serve as a coordinating center for total institutional planning and the evaluation of short-range and long-range implementation of established plans in the other four key areas.

Regardless of the organizational arrangement, the planning officer by himself cannot do all of the planning and evaluation. His job is to initiate actions and to see that the work of preparing alternate plans is done, that the components are kept in step, that the actions are taken in the correct sequence, and that the whole is put together into integrated short-range and long-range plans. He performs this kind of function in a staff capacity to the president, who has the responsibility of reviewing and approving all plans before they are presented to the governing board. The president should also have reporting directly to him an independent evaluator of program performance, who would also be located in the planning office. The development of sound educational policies and programs, together with the necessary physical plant and financing to achieve them, lies at the heart of academic planning. These policies and programs have to be accomplished by additional plans developed specifically in terms of present and future personnel requirements, physical facilities, equipment, and finances. From this brief description, it may be seen that planning is a part of the responsibilities of each of the key executive officers, as well as a major responsibility for the chief planning officer.

4. *Planning the Advancement Program*

The advancement program plan details the implementation of the institution's master plan; it should be in writing, and subject to frequent revision and refinement. It needs to be as specific and quantitative as possible and must be substantiated by the necessary budget. Total institutional planning and advancement program planning have to be done hand in hand since acquisition of private and public funds is so important in financing the master plan. The advancement program manager should provide the president with figures on gift potential and must be able to estimate the resources and length of time required to influence public opinion toward greater support.

When the long and short-term objectives have been agreed upon, the various advancement offices are in a position to submit projections on personnel, space, and support requirements. Clearly, program or project planning and budgeting make for a more effective advancement operation. Projects are planned to implement the institution's master plan and the necessary budgets are determined. Allocation of personnel services and other overhead can be made along with estimates of direct costs for the expected duration of the project—be it a one-shot special event or an intensive fund raising program. The more detailed the planning, the greater is the likelihood that each of the advancement program's officers will be in charge of his various projects and not merely responsive to them. To quote the old adage, prior planning prevents poor performance.

All activities within the institutional advancement program must have coordinated planning in order to avoid duplication and wasted resources. The act of planning is as important as implementation of the plans. Planning is a dynamic, on-going process and not a one-time activity. Realistic medium or long-range planning imposes discipline upon faculties and administrations. Traditionally these groups have been reluctant to engage in the detailed analytical work involved in setting sound goals, and yet they are interested in future policies, and can usually make a contribution to them. The better managed universities and colleges are eliminating, as far as possible, subjective guesses from their planning and are making great strides in using factual data to build and support their plans and programs. The beneficial results of systematic planning are available for all to see. There can no longer be any excuse for an institution's failure to plan on a sound basis its future goals, priorities, and allocation of resources.

B. The Evaluation Process

1. *Importance of Evaluation and Its Ingredients*

An advancement program must ultimately be evaluated with respect to achievement of the institution's educational objectives. The program is not an end in itself, only a method employed by the chief executive officers to attain understanding and support for the educational program objectives they have established. Evaluation is essential because without fairly precise knowledge of results, there can be no substantive planning.

Thad L. Hungate in *Management in Higher Education* (see Related Readings) defines evaluation as:

> ... the process of securing value judgments essential to the improvement of the services of the institution. These judgments may be based on objective evidence, on experience, on subjective judgment, or on any combination of the three. Such judgments seek to assess the suit-

ability or desirability of an activity or resource in relation both to institutional purpose and to cost. There can be no rational improvement in institutional services without the exercise of value judgments concerning all aspects of operations. Indeed every act of management reflects such judgments. The concern is to provide more adequate bases for them and hence increase their reliability.

Evaluation differs from pure measurement in that it is a comparison of results with objectives, of "X" amount of output with "Y" amount of input. Evaluation can either be quantitative or qualitative, objective or subjective. It may not always be possible, or desirable, to put evaluation in quantitative terms.

When quantitative assessments are possible, it may often be of more importance to the advancement program manager to evaluate his own organization's performance by analyzing trends, costs, productivity, and other factors according to individual programs than to compare his results with other institutions whose figures may be composed of unknown or dissimilar ingredients. It should be realized that absolute evaluation of an advancement program is impossible since financial and academic decisions can have a direct effect on the activities designed to advance the understanding and support of the institution. However, meaningful evaluations can still be made and should be the practice of every key person engaged in institutional advancement activities. Yet, unless the chief executive officers of the institution recognize the importance of systematic evaluation and its benefits, such analysis can be hampered by unsympathetic attitudes and the lack of necessary funds and staff time to do the job. Evaluation is an on-going, dynamic process, for as Hungate explains, "Because planning and operations are continuous functions, it follows that the process of evaluation must also be a continuous function."

Broadly speaking, there are four ingredients necessary for successful evaluation: (1) clear policies and objectives, (2) relevant institutional or personal standards of acceptable performance, (3) reliable data, and (4) systematic procedures. Each is interrelated with the others.

Policies and Objectives

Before any evaluation is possible, clear objectives and purposes need to be established. Operating policies will serve as guidelines, and performance can be evaluated against stated objectives.

Relevant Institutional and Personal Standards

Standards of acceptable performance are the byproduct of (a) measuring performance against objectives of various activities and (b) comparisons within and among institutions. Standards tend to be subjective and personal, and many performance standards are often subconscious, unless thought about carefully so the individual becomes aware of the process by which he judges performance. Over a period of time each institution and individual develops a minimum standard or level of performance that is tolerated. Objectives reflect not only aspirations or goals, but also standards which are historical in that they reflect cumulative performance in a given area by an institution or individual. Objectives stated in a language which is as precise and quantitative as possible tend to be more useful to the advancement program manager, but he must not overlook subjective standards of performance.

An evaluation of standards of acceptable performance begins with the purposes of the advancement program. Viewed as the manager would look at it, the broad purpose of the advancement program is to advance the understanding and support of the particular institution. Beyond this statement, each institution will need to develop the purposes of its own advancement program in more specific language. The more refined the objectives, and the more specific the time period and resources to be allocated, the easier and more accurate the evaluation. Generally stated objectives such as "more funds," "more students," or "more buildings" do not lend themselves to useful evaluation.

The establishment of long-range and short-range objectives as part of the overall institutional plan is an excellent method of avoiding the imprecision of generalized statements, and of keeping the all-important "down the pike" view. The long-range objectives of most institutional advancement programs could probably be defined very generally as *increased funds, community understanding,* and *recognition within the education profession.* These broad purposes, which have many implications, form the basis for more specific objectives that will depend upon the nature of the institution and the unique situation in which it currently finds itself. For example, the term *"increased funds"* usually gives the connotation that more gift dollars are required, but there could be a tuition increase which needs careful handling and explaining, or a requirement for more research funds from government and private sources, or an important briefing for the legislature which is considering the institution's appropriation.

Better *community understanding*—local, state, and regional—is always important. From a practical point of view, every institution must be conscious of zoning, sewage, public transportation laws, court decisions, traffic egress and ingress, and myriad other considerations in addition to its needs for financial support. Equally important are the philosophical considerations. A college or university as a part of a community has a responsibility to contribute to the cultural and social life of that community. It cannot separate itself and take the attitude that what is good for "X" university is, therefore, good for "Y" community. Also an institution of higher learning has to consider its role in the academic community of similar institutions, as well as its mission as part of the total educational apparatus of its community, state, and region.

Recognition within the education profession is important in recruiting the type of faculty and students required by the institution's objectives, in obtaining gifts and grants, and in building up that all-important prestige factor so difficult to measure.

Reliable Data

Information requirements vary among institutions and within departments of the same institution. The information retrieval system, therefore, should be specifically designed for the needs of the individual institution and its consumers since the scope, emphasis, staff, and budget for advancement programs vary widely.

In view of the progress of electronic data processing (EDP) technology, it is more practical and desirable than ever to consider using a central source for information storage and acquisition. The availability of data is more important than the location of the records-keeping machinery. Many institutions have or plan to install a centralized computer system. Ideally this system would also serve the needs of the institution's advancement program. Centralized systems are more efficient, but may not always be available at a moment's notice for some operations. Therefore, planning is required, and it should be possible for advancement program personnel to anticipate most requirements. Problems will be minimized if persons remember the sign which appears in an IBM office: "MAN: slow, slovenly, brilliant; IBM: fast, accurate, stupid."

If an institution does not have a computer on campus, or the EDP center is not available to the advancement program office, EDP service centers are expanding rapidly and most can handle any needs on a contract basis. The computer does not evaluate, but it does provide one method of information storage and acquisition. Great care should be exercised in deciding upon the amount and importance of information to be stored either on computer tape or in the old-fashioned file cabinet, so as not to waste money and storage space by keeping material that is not needed.

Systematic Procedures

The institution's chief executive officers need to recognize that evaluation is an important management tool and without it planning and implementation will be less effective. They also need to recognize that evaluation itself must be planned and implemented. A predetermined systematic procedure is necessary for stating objectives, establishing relevant standards, and collecting reliable data. The procedure for evaluation will be a product of the various individuals and offices directly concerned, such as the president, the academic vice president, the advancement program manager, the business office, and so forth. The procedure should be considerably formalized, well known to the parties concerned and periodically reviewed for possible improvements. Information requirements must also be subjected to revision, for unless there is a definite process for updating, acquisition of data can be a wasted exercise. The principle underlying the procedure for information collection is the need to insure that evaluative information, on time and in usable form, reaches the desired person so it can be incorporated into the decision-making process.

Before discussing evaluation of the advancement program as a total entity, it is helpful to consider evaluation of its component parts.

2. Evaluation of Fund Raising Activities

The quest for private gift dollars is consuming an ever-increasing portion of an institution's resources in time, money, and personnel.

Effective evaluation is imperative for sound management of these fund raising activities. Findings reported in Chapter II indicate that gift income—excluding deferred gifts, such as bequests, life income trusts and agreements, gift annuities, and life insurance contracts—is a fairly reliable indicator of total gifts, without being distorted by annual fluctuations. If an institution conducts a fairly extensive deferred gifts program, it might want to deduct its expenditures for this program when comparing over the short haul its costs with gift income to determine its gift dollar costs.

Establishing a Set of Indicators

Although all analyses in the reported study were based on three-year average figures, reliability of the indicators will only be established over a period of time. In the interim, it is suggested that an individual institutional advancement program construct its own profile of indicators to include:

a. total gifts (defined in Chapter II)

b. gifts, excluding bequests and other deferred gifts such as annuities, life income agreements, trusts, and insurance contracts

c. advancement program expenditures according to the cost of each activity, i.e., fund raising, alumni relations, information services (excluding publications), publications (including cost of publications prepared and used specifically for the advancement program), and other activities (separate accounting is preferred if there are major items, such as federal or state liaison, central services, and university press)

d. educational and general expenditures of the institution*

e. advancement expenditures ("c" above) as a percent of gifts ("b" above)

f. gifts ("b" above) as a percent of educational and general expenditures ("d" above)

---

* The educational and general expenditures (E&G) are as defined in *College and University Business Administration*, American Council on Education, Washington, D. C., 1968.

g. advancement expenditures ("c" above) as a percent of educational and general expenditures ("d" above)

h. gifts from alumni (excluding deferred gifts) as a percent of "b"

i. percentage of alumni contributing to those solicited

j. number of cultivation calls and solicitation calls made by (1) trustees, (2) president, and (3) volunteers

k. number of organizations and individuals solicited by same categories in which gift income records are kept

l. number of organizations and individuals making contributions by same categories in which gift income records are kept.

Other indicators appropriate to a particular institution or to a particular project can be added.

Use of Indicators

As gauges of performance, and as warning signs to management that some activity may not be moving along as planned, indicators can be of value. They are also of value for planning purposes and in allocating resources by management. However, indicators are only that and should never be considered as absolute measures. There is no "correct" percentage of educational and general expenditures which should be allocated to the advancement program. Neither is there an optimum gift dollar cost. Each indicator will vary according to management's decisions as to what is desirable, and according to the unique characteristics of the particular institution.

Indicators become meaningful when compared with some predetermined base. Thus a college or university may determine in its long-range planning that it must double gift income by a certain year and continue the increase thereafter by some established percentage. The management decision is how much to expend for a given situation. It is expected that the initial start-up expenditures for personnel and program will be a higher proportion of the E&G amount than had been previously experienced. Some estimates have been made about the duration of this higher outlay. The chief executive officers have also calculated their past performance in fund raising relative to expenditures. Therefore, they have guidelines as to what levels of outlay and performance are appropriate at certain stages of the gift income programs. As a result, deviations can be detected and corrected.

It is worthwhile to illustrate with another example the warning signals indicators can give. Institutions which expend more on their advancement programs than they receive in gifts (there were two in the study sample and the situation is not rare) should use this indicator as a warning that analysis of, and justification for, such expenditure is needed. Likewise, if cost per gift dollar appears extremely low, the managers will probably want to check their accounting practices to be sure the figures reflect costs accurately. Gifts are not free; it costs money to raise money. Perhaps certain costs are being overlooked, giving the institution a deceptively favorable picture of a program. An accurate picture is greatly to be preferred, as it is likely to stimulate improvement and lead to actual attainment of what was erroneously thought of as attained. However, it should be remembered that indicators are gauges, not sacrosanct boundaries which prohibit bold actions.

Gift categories as developed by the Council for Financial Aid to Education seem to be quite adequate for accounting purposes in most cases. The recommended gift categories are:

General welfare foundations
Business corporations
Alumni
Non-alumni individuals
Religious organizations
Non-alumni, non-church groups
Other sources

In some situations, institutions may want to expand one or more of the categories to include sources of funds specific to their particular kind of institution, for example, gifts from a number of religious groups or a fund raising association of independent colleges.

Accounting Procedures and Maintenance of Records

In keeping an account of the cost of programs, the breakdown of expenditures should be no more detailed than necessary to facilitate adequate controls and planning. Since the purpose is to isolate specific operations for more reliable evaluation, it is recommended that, as often as possible, expenditures be kept on a project basis, e.g., annual fund, "X" special event, operation of regional offices, specific publications (including postage and handling).

In addition to expenditures which can be recorded by a direct cost allocation or charging system, there are many advancement program activities for which costs are not now allocated specifically and accurately. Of these activities, some lend themselves more appropriately to regular accounting procedures than do others. For example, if an institution's trustees, president, and key faculty actively participate in fund raising activities, their time is not usually charged on a prorated basis. To allocate the time of these key officers accurately to each of the activities involved would require an accounting system of much greater complexity than seems warranted. As an acceptable compromise, it is suggested that an informal accounting at the end of each year be made by means of a memorandum, in which the proportion of time spent by these key officers on advancement program activities is estimated. This would not be a part of the regular accounting system; rather, it would be a special analysis which would permit more realistic estimates of the actual costs of raising funds, conducting public relations programs, and carrying out alumni relations activities.

Monthly computations of gift income by source, as well as expenditures by departments and activities, is a recommended procedure. Monthly compilation enables results for any specified period of time to be compared with another period, thereby providing feedback information to the advancement program manager with reasonable frequency. Expenditure and income figures should be provided within 10 days of the end of the preceding month to be of maximum use.

Evaluation requirements will dictate some of the information requirements of the fund raising office. Complete donor files should be maintained, together with files for prospective donors. Sources and amount of wealth, composition of assets, family information, specific connections with the institution, philanthropic activities, special interests, and visits with the donor by institutional personnel are some of the items of information which should be maintained about every important, or prospectively important, donor. Special file folders on the most important donors and prospects may be desirable. The reason for itemizing specifically the above information is that determining gift potential is one of the key factors in evaluating the probable success of present and future fund raising programs. Gift potential determination can become a useful management tool when information about gift potential from all sources is compared with opinion samples and institutional gift objectives. Over a period of years, systematic fact-finding and careful analysis of performance can be added to professional intuition to provide reliable evaluative and planning data.

If each institution would maintain the necessary records for evaluating performance, the effectiveness and efficiency of fund raising in higher education would be significantly improved. Through use of the previously discussed indicators, performance yardsticks could gradually be developed which would permit realistic comparisons among and within institutions.

3. *Evaluating the Public Relations Program*

The public relations office is essentially responsible for maintaining contact with communications media, with the community (in both the broader and narrower sense), and with the institution's faculty, staff, students, and other concerned groups. To accomplish its objectives, the public relations office develops specific projects as part of the overall advancement program. The more specific the project, the more specific the purposes usually are, and the more reliable the evaluation tends to be.

Findings from the study on which this report is based indicate movement in the direction of a more scientific approach in the evaluations institutions make of their public relations activities.

Intuition has been a key factor in the management of most college public relations programs, but increasing costs and demands on the program will not permit continuation of subjective assessment of results. Measurements of the effectiveness of public relations activities are becoming more objective and quantitative as a result of the interest of social scientists in this field. Motivational research, opinion studies, and content analyses are providing analytical techniques to replace the scrap book and subjective rationalizations of practitioners. Opinion research and sampling can be quite effective when planned and implemented by a skillful researcher, and few colleges are without one or more such qualified persons who could offer guidance in setting up such a program.

Even with the emerging interest of the social scientist, evaluation of public relations activities is still far from scientific. Evaluation can be enhanced, however, by the establishment of multiple-project programs—programs composed of a number of small projects, such as special events and promotional campaigns, each with its own built-in specific purposes and evaluative criteria. With programs divided into sub-components, objectives are often more specifically stated, facilitating analysis of the extent to which they are achieved.

Evaluation, or measurements of effectiveness, can be accomplished by a number of methods. The most obvious is, of course, by analyzing the results quantitatively. This method is most effective with short-term projects. The selection of what should be "counted" in evaluating results requires astuteness and sometimes ingenuity, and appropriate choices will differ from activity to activity. For example, special events lend themselves to quantitative measurement, but true evaluation goes beyond attendance figures in seeking to determine to what degree the event accomplished its purposes.

A variation of clipping counting can be used to provide partial evaluation of the success of the institution's information activities. But since establishing a certain attitude in the minds of certain individuals is the ultimate objective of most public relations activities, the type of story and media concerned are more important than total column inches. Publication of a certain type of story sometimes can be more effective in county weeklies than in the *New York Times*.

Properly speaking each item should have a pre-designed purpose, audience, and media, as this generally insures greater effectiveness. Measurement can thus take into consideration these three factors, but an additional piece of information is necessary, before evaluation is possible. This consists of the item's impact. Just because an item gets past the media "gatekeepers" does not mean it has impact or effect. Opinion research is one common measurement tool for determining what influence a news story, radio program, film, or similar public relations item has had. Nonetheless, in some cases, determining the impact or effect of a particular item is often difficult if not impossible. However, over a period of time, opinion research can help in evaluating the effectiveness of information releases designed for a specific purpose, audience, and media. Therefore, managers might be well advised to conduct opinion analyses at regular intervals to collect base data and measure subsequent changes.

Opinion research is an important tool since it can provide the institution with feedback about the results of its activities. Other techniques are also important. Techniques such as visitors and speakers bureaus (along with periodic surveys) are useful for feedback, if there has been established a formal system of "debriefing"—a process which extracts specific answers and impressions from visitors and speakers. Procedures for obtaining feedback should be built into every possible public relations activity. Questionnaires, interviews, news stories, letters, and even informal conversational groups are among the sources of information which offer excellent opportunities for feedback.

Another measurement tool is content analysis. It can provide a quantitative and objective description of various aspects of the content of publications and news releases. Relatively simple content analysis of releases and publications will help determine whether there is consistency between established objectives and actual content. Researchers familiar with content analysis procedures are available in the psychology, sociology, or journalism faculties of many institutions. The public relations practitioner will benefit from knowing something about what content analysis techniques can achieve.

It will be found that public relations activities can be better adapted to a dynamic environment when there is (1) regular evaluation and (2) maintenance of flexibility in the use of personnel. Particular institutional situations will dictate the degree of specialization and the assignments necessary. The more versatile the staff members, the more easily a public relations director will be able to use his personnel in a variety of capacities and to focus his staff on new and different projects. Personnel with wider ranges of talents, therefore, offer greater flexibility. This can be a considerable asset because evaluation may indicate the need for shifts in emphasis, or development of new programs to meet changing requirements. Evolving social conditions will also force other alterations of the institution's advancement program activities.

4. *Evaluating the Alumni Program*

The study findings upon which this report draws indicate that alumni activities are conducted in as many different ways as are public relations programs. Some institutions separate alumni relations activities from fund raising, and some do not. A pattern in the size of staffs of alumni relations offices was detected (Chapter II), as was a tendency for institutions which conducted alumni fund raising as part of the development office operation to receive more gift dollars from alumni (again see Chapter II). Research over a period of years will be required to elaborate and substantiate these initial findings.

There are few measurement tools which have any degree of widespread use in the evaluation of non-fund raising activities conducted by the alumni program. Gift income, of course, is commonly used as one way to evaluate alumni fund raising efforts. Means of assessment vary with institutions, and one alumni program is not necessarily comparable to another at a similar institution. Over the long run, however, certain measurements and ratios should begin to appear within a single institution's program that would give its management guidelines for evaluation. It may be that gift dollar production is a reliable benchmark of the total alumni program, but further research will be required before this concept can be generalized as applying to all institutions. In the meantime, it is advisable for each advancement program manager and alumni administrator to work toward the establishment of performance figures for his own institution.

Many myths surround alumni fund raising in terms of what constitutes performance in this area. For example, percentage of alumni contributing is meaningless as a figure for comparison between institutions until standard definitions for alumni are widely employed. However, the percentage of successful solicitations has some significance, and, properly handled, participation percentages can be useful stimulants to both staff and donor. The study found that cost per alumnus gift dollar decreased as gift dollars from alumni increased (see Chapter II). This suggests that, although participation is important, exhortations for increases in participation percentages should not be made at the expense of appeals for increased level of giving. As one college president pointed out, "Participation is not legal tender!" Some of the larger potential donors believe alumni participation to be indicative of overall financial support of the institution. The fact that universities, both public and private, tended in the study sample to have lower participation percentages than colleges, although they did better in fund raising, might indicate this belief is not necessarily true.

The use of average alumnus gift figures can have the same sight-lowering effect upon the donor as participation percentage appeals. In other words, the donor might "just give something" to help the percentage figures or contribute the "average" amount when he might be capable of far greater support. On the other hand, such figures may encourage some donors to give who would not do so otherwise. Yet, if it is concluded that these contributions would only be token ones, a trade-off of smaller gifts from the majority of donors in order to include "token" donors would be a mistake. The point of this discussion is that management tools such as participation percentage and average gift figures (if the institution is convinced that they are proven evaluative criteria) may or may not be appropriate as promotional tools, depending upon the situation and its objectives.

Information criteria and maintenance of records are the same for alumni as for the fund raising office. One exception is that more information concerning college activities, academic programs, and degrees granted will probably be needed about each alumnus.

Techniques similar to those used to evaluate public relations activities are applicable. The effects of alumni special events should be evaluated, as well as those activities designed for general public relations with the alumni. All such activities need to be subjected to systematic, objective analysis designed to eliminate, as far as possible, emotional judgment. Certain programs and special events have a way of becoming "traditional" overnight.

5. *Evaluating the Publications Effort*

An institution's production of publications is not a program in itself any more than a particular publication is an end in itself. Both the program and the individual publications exist as components of other programs or projects. This point is often overlooked in the proliferation of educational printed matter. Publications, as spoken of in this section, do not include books from university presses or scholarly works by faculty and staff, but refer to materials which are produced with the expressed intention of advancing understanding and support of the institution. Each institution should strive to make its publications, from annual report to promotional flyer, representative of an educational institution of high quality. They should be concise and well written (honesty is assumed). Graphics and design must be attractive and be aids to readability and usability, not hindrances.

Few publications offices are involved with the production of all publications disseminated by the institution. Most of them are concerned with producing publications in the general advancement program area. Some operate their own printing presses, but the majority contract jobs to commercial suppliers. Ideally, the publications office is operated on a self-sustaining basis, i.e., printing costs, office services, and overhead are allocated directly to the initiating department. The university editor, or director of publications, should report to the manager of the advancement program and coordinate all the institution's publications. He and his office should lend technical assistance to other institutional offices in editing, copy preparation, layout and design, photography, printing production, and distribution.

Evaluation of a publications office tends to be subjective, but evaluation of the effectiveness of particular publications should have greater objectivity and be viewed in the framework of the specific program they support. As part of a project, a publication serves particular objectives and has a role to play. It is in this context that the publication must be evaluated. A portion of the printed material produced by a publications office is of service variety—forms, information folders, and directives. Utility is the chief criterion for this type of printed matter. On the other hand, major publications, such as catalogs, brochures and promotional material, readily lend themselves to periodic evaluation. It goes without saying, of course, that even before publication such materials are first appraised and pretested.

Three factors enter evaluation of publications:

1. objectives of the publication relative to the program or project of which it is a part

2. content analysis of the material within the publication to be sure content is consistent with objectives

3. data about responses to publications, obtained by surveys, interviews, and other means

As yet, relatively few institutions subject their publications to evaluation. Only a handful of universities have attempted to evaluate the effectiveness of all or any group of institutional publications. However, most institutions have a number of faculty members qualified to conduct or supervise content analysis, surveys, and interview procedures. Regular publications, such as magazines and newsletters, should undergo periodically a rigorous assessment employing all three of the above evaluation criteria. Special publications—such as development brochures, promotional literature for special events, and internal publications—can be analyzed individually or as a group.

Some Concluding Comments About Evaluating Advancement Programs

The broad purpose of an institutional advancement program, as defined in this report, is to advance the understanding and support of the particular institution. Long-term objectives of most institutional advancement programs can probably be designated as increased funds, community understanding, and professional recognition. To be effective, the various activities involved in achieving these objectives must complement each other. The sum of the parts is not necessarily the desired whole, because each activity could be effective according to its own self-established objectives, but the objectives of one activity could be at cross-purposes with another. For this reason, the manager of the advancement program needs to establish coordinated planning procedures and to develop the organizational structure necessary to do the job.

It is difficult at this point to offer criteria for evaluating advancement programs that will be equally appropriate for all institutions of higher learning. The mix of ingredients, and the importance of the various programs, will vary with the relative degree of importance of the three objectives. If *increased funds* far overshadows *community understanding* and *professional recognition* in importance, gift dollars would naturally be the central measurement factor of performance.

Increased funds help attract better faculty and a better physical plant, which help attract better administrative leadership, all of which help provide a better academic program, which in turn helps attract more money. It is like a circle of interrelationships in which one relationship is dependent upon the others. The trend in financing individual institutions of higher education appears to be some combination of private, state, and federal funds. There is still a sizable differential in tuition between state and private institutions, but should a greater flow of state and federal scholarship funds be legislated the gap could be reduced. Currently, the pressure is on the federal government to spread among a larger number of institutions research funds and incentive grants designed to strengthen certain academic areas. Eventually, state aid to private institutions will be an accepted procedure and will become a significant dollar source.

As time progresses and patterns for financing educational institutions are altered, educational dollars from both private and tax sources will become increasingly competitive, and therefore these dollars may become the principal measuring factor of advancement program productivity. It is still premature to offer a statement as to the composition of the sources of income which would be the objective of a concerted effort on the part of the institution's advancement program staff. At this juncture, when an institution places its emphasis on the first objective—*increased funds*—use of private gift dollars as a measuring tool will provide an accurate indicator. But as an ever-increasing portion of the advancement program effort is spent on "total" financing, new indicators will have to be incorporated for effective evaluation.

An impression was gained from the study findings presented in this report that most of the institutions which were receiving a substantial amount of gift dollars focused most of their advancement program activities, directly and indirectly, on the securing of these gift dollars. For such institutions, evaluation relative to gift income presents a fairly accurate assessment of advancement program productivity. A strong argument could be made that, with minor variations, *increased funds* should be the ultimate objective of all advancement programs. Admittedly, this is an oversimplification of the underlying purposes of the advancement program, but to attempt to examine every kind of fund raising activity in its proper perspective would present an extremely complicated picture that would defy evaluation. To pursue the hypothesis that *increased funds* is the ultimate objective of every advancement program activity, consider the fact that sound projects designed to further *community understanding* and *professional recognition* will eventually result in increased funding if the fund raising department follows through on the opportunities.

Maintaining effective communication and establishing the best possible relationships with the various publics will largely be wasted if:

• the fund raising department is not alert for gift support,

• the admissions office does not follow through with effective student recruitment contacts,

• the legislative liaison office is not keeping abreast of specific legislation and of fostering the interest of legislators concerned with the institution's needs,

• the president and deans are not offering leadership in the recruiting and maintaining of a quality faculty and academic program.

At this early stage in the development of meaningful evaluative criteria for advancement programs of institutions of higher learning, the amount and cost of gift dollars appear the best measurement of productivity for many institutions, state and private, college and university. It will be realized that certain advancement activities, though desirable, well administered, and effective, may have only tangential results in the fund raising program. Institutions must make special management decisions regarding these activities, and, if the activities are to be continued, institutions must realize that gift dollars as a portion of advancement program expenditures might cost a bit more than those of some other similar institution. There is nothing wrong with this type of management decision because, as mentioned before, there is no ironclad optimal ratio of expenses to income. With further refinement and experience in the use of evaluative procedures, gift income will surely be expanded to include other revenues as a gauge for productivity of the advancement program and, likewise, analysis of expenditures will undergo a similar process of development.

RELATED READINGS

Burns, Gerald P., ed. *Administrators in Higher Education*. New York: Harper & Row, 1962.

Corson, John J. *Governance of Colleges and Universities*. New York: McGraw-Hill Book Company, 1960.

Dodds, Harold. *The Academic President—Educator or Caretaker*. New York: McGraw-Hill Book Company, 1962.

Dressel, Paul L. *Evaluation in Higher Education*. Boston: Houghton Mifflin Company, 1961.

Drucker, Peter. *The Effective Executive*. New York: Harper & Row, 1967.

Gibson, Raymond C. *The Challenge of Leadership in Higher Education*. Dubuque, Iowa: Wm. C. Brown Company, 1964.

Harris, Seymour E., ed. *Challenge and Change in American Education*. Berkeley, California: McCutchan Publishing Corp., 1965.

———. *Higher Education: Resources and Finance*. New York: McGraw-Hill Book Company, 1962.

Hungate, Thad L. *Management in Higher Education*. New York: Bureau of Publications, Teachers College, Columbia University, 1964.

Keezer, Dexter, ed. *Financing Higher Education, 1960-70*. New York: McGraw-Hill Book Company, 1959.

Likert, Rensis. *New Patterns of Management*. New York: McGraw-Hill Book Company, 1961.

Millett, John D. *The Academic Community: An Essay on Organization*. New York: McGraw-Hill Book Company, 1962.

Rourke, Francis, and Glenn Brooks. *The Managerial Revolution in Higher Education*. Baltimore, Maryland: Johns Hopkins Press, 1966.

Stoke, Harold. *The American College President*. New York: Harper and Brothers, 1959.

Tickton, Sidney G. *Needed—A Ten Year College Budget*. New York: The Fund for the Advancement of Education, 1961.

Williams, Harry. *Planning for Effective Resource Allocation in Universities*. Washington: American Council on Education, 1966.

The Advancement of Understanding and Support of Higher Education. Washington: American College Public Relations Association, 1958. (Available on microfiche.)

APPENDIX A:

Questionnaire Used in Study

NEW TRENDS

IN PUBLIC RELATIONS AND FUND RAISING

AT U. S. COLLEGES AND UNIVERSITIES

A Study Conducted by the American College Public Relations Association

Name of Institution _____

Enrollment:

Undergraduates (F. T. E.)   _____

Graduate students (F. T. E.)   _____

Total (F. T. E.)   _____

Type of control: public _____ private _____

Check one of the following which most nearly defines your institution:

Major private university   _____

Public institution state controlled   _____

Private men's college   _____

Private women's college   _____

Private coeducational college   _____

Professional/specialized institute   _____

Municipal college or university   _____

Junior or community (2-year) college   _____

Section I Organizational Patterns

Since World War II pressures have built up to bring about a number of organizational patterns in higher educational administration. This is especially true in the overall area of institutional development and advancement.

Some organizational charts look like this:

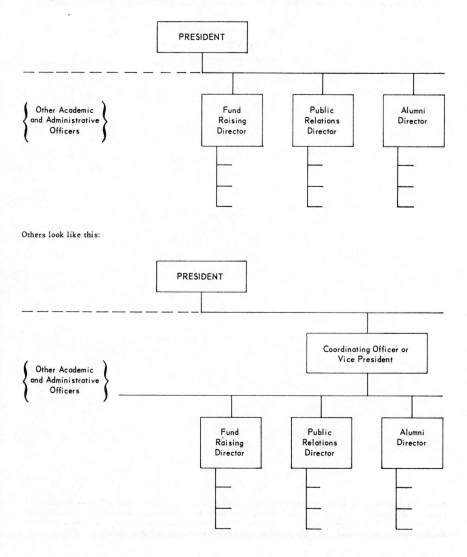

Others look like this:

We are interested in your concepts of management, and request that you complete as many as possible of the following charts.

Chart 1

Please draw your own institution's current organization chart insofar as it relates to public relations, publications, fund raising and alumni affairs; carry it down to, but not including, secretaries, student and clerical helpers.

```
┌─────────────────┐
│    PRESIDENT    │
└─────────────────┘
```

Note: Of the person(s) in the above chart reporting directly to the president, please mark a "1" in the box of the person(s) who is/are directly and officially involved in the major decision-making process of the institution; mark a "2" in the box of the person(s) who is/are consulted on decisions affecting his area only; and mark a "3" in the box of the person(s) who serve(s) as a staff person to implement previously arrived-at decisions.

Chart 2

If possible and if different, please draw your own institution's organization chart which was used prior to the adoption of the one given in chart 1 on the previous page. Again, please relate the chart only to the public relations, fund raising, alumni affairs and publications; carry it down to, but not including, secretaries, student and clerical helpers.

This organizational chart was replaced by the one on the previous page in _____.

                                                                        (year)

```
┌─────────────────────┐
│     PRESIDENT       │
└─────────────────────┘
```

Note: Of the person(s) in the above chart reporting directly to the president, please mark a "1" in the box of the person(s) who is/are directly and officially involved in the major decision-making process of the institution; mark a "2" in the box of the person(s) who is/are consulted on decisions affecting his area only; and mark a "3" in the box of the person(s) who serve(s) as a staff person to implement previously arrived-at decisions.

Chart 3

If you anticipate, or are planning, any reorganization in the public relations, fund raising, alumni or publications areas, please draw the changes below. This reorganization should be completed by _____.

(year)

```
┌─────────────────┐
│   PRESIDENT     │
└─────────────────┘
```

Note: Of the person(s) in the above chart reporting directly to the president, please mark a "1" in the box of the person(s) who is/are directly and officially involved in the major decision-making process of the institution; mark a "2" in the box of the person(s) who is/are consulted on decisions affecting his area only; and.mark a "3" in the box of the person(s) who serve(s) as a staff person to implement previously arrived-at decisions.

Chart 4

If charts 1, 2, or 3 are not what you would consider an ideal organizational structure, and if personalities, individual strengths and weaknesses, traditions, etc., did not have to be considered, what would be your ideal *functional* organization of the overall institutional development and advancement area?

```
┌─────────────────────┐
│     PRESIDENT       │
└─────────────────────┘
```

Note: Of the person(s) in the above chart reporting directly to the president, please mark a "1" in the box of the person(s) who is/are directly and officially involved in the major decision-making process of the institution; mark a "2" in the box of the person(s) who is/are consulted on decisions affecting his area only; and mark a "3" in the box of the person(s) who serve(s) as a staff person to implement previously arrived-at decisions.

Mr. President:

The questions on this page and next are among the most important in the survey. Neither of the two major salary studies (soon to be one because the U.S. Office of Education has just announced it is suspending its survey for at least a year) is adequate in this area of education administration. It is essential to get complete and accurate answers, and, for this reason, this questionnaire is strictly confidential.

On the other hand, we do intend to publish salary and budget ranges for the various types of institutions. This information will, we think, be quite valuable to you. We urge you, therefore, to see that the questions on these two pages are answered fully and with care.

You may wish to have this section filled out by the chief personnel and/or business officer. It is recognized that the chart on the following page may not be adequate for the entire professional staff of larger institutions, so please attach an extra sheet of paper to this section.

Total Public Relations Budget (including salaries) $_____

Total Alumni Office Budget (including salaries) $_____

Total Fund Raising Budget (including salaries) $_____

_____ $_____

_____ $_____

_____ $_____

_____ $_____

_____ $_____

    Total $_____

Is Publications budget included in the above budgets? Yes _____ No _____

If yes, under which budget(s)? _____

If no, what is amount (including salaries) $_____

In the following chart the last three columns cover salary ranges. Rather than dollar figures, use the letter which corresponds in the following table:

A. $25,000 & above
B. $20,000 to $24,999
C. $17,500 to $19,999
D. $15,000 to $17,499

E. $12,500 to $14,999
F. $10,000 to $12,499
G. $5,000 to $9,999
H. Under $5,000

Note: Please consider straight salary, excluding all fringe benefits.

	It Not Full Time Write In Fraction	Check If Alumnus	Highest Degree	Years Employed Here	Salary Ranges (for position, not person)		
					60-61	62-63	64-65
Chief Coordinating Officer (if applicable) Title _____							
Chief Public Relations Officer Title _____							
Public Relations Staff: Title _____							
Title _____							
Title _____							
Title _____							
Title _____							
Chief Fund Raising Officer Title _____							
Fund Raising Staff: Title _____							
Title _____							
Title _____							
Title _____							
Title _____							
Chief Alumni Officer Title _____							
Alumni Staff: Title _____							
Title _____							
Title _____							
Title _____							
Title _____							
Chief Publications Officer Title _____							
Publications Staff: Title _____							
Title _____							
Title _____							

_____

Name of Institution

NEW TRENDS

IN PUBLIC RELATIONS AND FUND RAISING

AT U. S. COLLEGES AND UNIVERSITIES

A Study Conducted by the American College Public Relations Association

Section II Public Relations

1. What is the function, broadly conceived, of the public relations office of your institution?

2. Following are some of the categories of a public relations program.   What proportion of the time of the office's professional staff is devoted to:

   (1) Preparing releases for newspapers:

   Hometown   _____ %

   General news   _____ %

   Feature   _____ %

   (2) Releases for radio-TV   _____ %

   (3) Servicing national news media   _____ %

   (4) Community/regional relations (special events, liaison with local groups, etc.)   _____ %

   (5) Publications (see questions 3 and 4 on next page)   _____ %

   (6) Other: (please describe)   _____ %

3. What is the Public Relations Office budget, including salaries and publications?   _____

4. a. Excluding the direct cost (printing, art, production) of publications, what is the approximate budget of the Publication Office(s)?

   $_____

   b. Is this figure included in the amount listed in question 3? Yes _____ No _____

   c. What is the approximate annual amount spent on publications? $_____

5. What office or person is responsible for the following publications:

	Preparation of Copy (name of office)	Production (name of office)
Catalog	———————	———————
Annual report	———————	———————
Admissions materials	———————	———————
Alumni magazine	———————	———————
All-university magazine	———————	———————
Fund-raising materials	———————	———————
Student publications	———————	———————
Faculty-staff news bulletins	———————	———————
University press (book publishing)	———————	———————
Learned journals	———————	———————
Other	———————	———————

6. Direct mail is an important medium of communication. Please fill in the chart below in approximate round figures. Lists will overlap and duplicate, so please fill in the last question below the box.

Groups Receiving Mailing	Number in each group	What Materials Sent		How Handled: Addressograph, IBM, labels, etc.
		Public Relations	Fund Raising	
Alumni				
Students				
Faculty-Staff				
Donors				
Prospects (non-alumni)				
Parents				
Newspapers				
Athletic Sponsors				

7. What is the total number on your mailing lists? _____

NEW TRENDS

IN PUBLIC RELATIONS AND FUND RAISING

AT U. S. COLLEGES AND UNIVERSITIES

A Study Conducted by the American College Public Relations Association

Section III Fund-Raising Activities

A large part of an institution's efforts is directed toward achieving understanding and support of its educational program. This portion of the questionnaire deals with fund raising and one aspect of fund raising is the solicitation call.

Let's define a solicitation call as (a) a personal face-to-face talk (not as part of a group meeting) between a college representative and a prospect, in which (b) a specific gift (not "your interest and support") is openly and explicitly asked for. Solicitation calls are a lot easier to measure than "cultivation" or "communication." Remembering that this questionnaire is confidential, and that the replies will help each of us gain better perspective on his own efforts, please try to estimate as closely as possible in answering the following questions:

1. a. How many actual solicitation calls does your president make in an average 30-day period?*   _____

    b. How many actual solicitation calls does your typical "active" trustee or member of your governing board (you must define "active" yourself, but you don't need to spell it out) make in an average 30-day period?   _____

    How many actual solicitation calls does your typical "less-active" trustee or board member make in an average 30-day period?   _____

    What per cent of your trustees or board members is "active?"   _____ %

    c. How many actual solicitation calls do all your other unpaid volunteer workers (parents, class secretaries, businessmen and other support group members) combined make in an average 30-day period?   _____

    How many workers does it take to make that number of solicitation calls?   _____

    What per cent of the total number of volunteer workers is active in this way? _____ %

    d. How many actual solicitation calls does a typical "active" faculty member make in a month?   _____

    What per cent of faculty members does this?   _____ %

    e. How many actual solicitation calls(alone, and not accompanying a volunteer)does your entire salaried fund-raising staff make in an average 30-day period?   _____

    How many salaried staff persons does it take to make that number of calls?   _____

    How many times in an average 30-day period do salaried staff go out on solicitation calls with a president, trustee or volunteer?   _____

*Since intensive capital campaigns increase the level of activity, the term "30-day period" should reflect the *average* monthly activity over several years, which may have included a major campaign.

2. Please indicate the fund-raising budget (including salaries and publications).

1963-64 $_____; 1964-65 $_____; 1965-66 $_____

3. Private Gift Support: (include religious denomination grants, **but exclude all federal facilities grants and contracts and state general appropriations).** Include _only_ paid-up portions of pledges.

    a. How many bequests did your school receive from January 1, 1960 to December 31, 1964? _____

       For a dollar total of? $_____

    b. How many capital gifts (gifts for buildings or endowment) did your school receive from living people or existing organizations from January 1, 1960 to December 31, 1964? _____

       For a dollar total of? $_____

    c. How many gifts for current support (to be expended completely, now or in the next few years) came on your books from January 1, 1960 to December 31, 1964? _____

       For a dollar total of? $_____

    d. How many alumni contributions to the annual fund (not for capital gifts) came in from January 1, 1960, to December 31, 1964? (These gifts should be _included_ in part "c" above.) _____

       For a dollar total of? $_____

    e. How many annuity agreements did your school enter into from January 1, 1960 to December 31, 1964? _____

       Total corpus $_____

       Gift portion $_____

    f. How many life income and trust agreements did your school enter into from January 1, 1960 to December 31, 1964? _____

       Total corpus $_____

       Gift portion $_____

4. Which, if any, of the following are included in compiling your annual or regular gift income reports?

	Yes	No		Yes	No
Foundation Research Grants	_____	_____	Corporate Research Contracts	_____	_____
Foundation Research Contracts	_____	_____	Government Research Grants	_____	_____
Corporate Research Grants	_____	_____	Government Research Contracts	_____	_____

5. Are gifts-in-kind, such as books, art objects, equipment etc., reported as cash equivalents in annual report totals? Yes _____ No _____

<u>Name of Institution</u>

NEW TRENDS

IN PUBLIC RELATIONS AND FUND RAISING

AT U. S. COLLEGES AND UNIVERSITIES

A Study Conducted by the American College Public Relations Association

Section IV Alumni Affairs

1. What is your institution's definition of an alumnus?

2. a. What is your institution's estimated total number of living alumni? _____

   b. What is your institution's approximate number of up-to-date mailing addresses? _____

3. Is your institution's alumni organization legally independent?

                    Yes _____   No _____

4. a. Is your institution's alumni organization financially independent?

                    Yes _____   No _____

   b. What is the average cost per year of operating alumni activities? _____

   c. What per cent of this is supported by institutional funds? _____

5. a. Does the alumni organization have membership dues?

                    Yes _____   No _____

   b. If yes, how much are the dues?

                    annually $ _____; lifetime $_____ ; other $_____

   c. What is the average annual income from dues? $ _____

   From how many dues-paying members? _____

6. a. Is fund raising (other than dues) part of the responsibility of the alumni office?

    Yes_____   No_____

    b. If yes, what is a typical dollar amount for alumni annual giving?   _____

    c. What per cent of total staff time (all paid employees) is spent in this kind of fund raising in a typical year?

    _____

    d. In your estimation, approximately what per cent of donors is reached by personal face-to-face solicitation by

    either staff or alumni volunteers?   _____

7. a. What is the alumni office operating budget, including salaries and publications? $_____

    b. What are the titles of the professional staff people assigned to the alumni office?

Title	If not full time give percentage

8. Does your institution have an

	Yes	No	Frequency Published	Office Where Edited
Alumni Magazine	_____	_____	_____	_____
Alumni Newspaper	_____	_____	_____	_____
Other Alumni Publications	_____	_____	_____	_____

9. Does the lay alumni board exercise any veto power over:

    (1) editorial content of magazine

    Yes_____   No_____

    (2) alumni program activities

    Yes_____   No_____

    (3) alumni fund raising activities

    Yes_____   No_____

APPENDIX B:

Tables Showing Advancement Staff and Salary Statistics

TABLE 1
Advancement Program Staff Summary
(1967-68 Academic Year)

Type of Institution	Number of Institutions Reporting	Advancement Program Managers	Information Services			Publications			Fund Raising			Alumni			TOTALS
			Chief Officers	Staff Members	Totals	Chief Officers	Staff Members	Totals	Chief Officers	Staff Members	Totals	Chief Officers	Staff Members	Totals	
Private Universities	21	17	19	63	82	14	28	42	20	95	115	19	37	56	312
Private Coed	165	94	143	126	269	14	—	14	93	142	235	135	28	163	775
Private Men's	28	20	26	23	49	5	2	7	16	27	43	26	6	32	151
Private Women's	42	14	39	14	53	3	—	3	21	16	37	35	10	45	152
State Universities	42	21	38	184	222	20	43	63	28	42	70	38	54	92	468
State Colleges	80	12	80	67	147	14	2	16	18	6	24	36	2	38	237
Totals	378	178	345	477	822	70	75	145	196	328	524	289	137	426	2,095

Notes to Table:

1. All figures represent separate individuals. There are no duplications of individuals listed in the various functions even though some may have overlapping responsibilities.

2. By definition, an advancement program manager has responsibility for at least three of the four principal activities.

3. A number of advancement program managers are also immediately responsible for one of the specific functions, typically fund raising or public relations, in addition to coordinating and directing the other activities. In such cases, the individual will not be listed as the chief fund raising or public relations officer.

4. All number are for professional staff persons. No secretaries are listed.

TABLE 2

Advancement Programs

Professional Staffs

1967-68 Academic Year
(378 Institutions)

Number of Staff Members	Private Universities	Private Coed	Private Men's	Private Women's	State Universities	State Colleges
1		3		4		20
2		18		9	1	19
3		33	4	8	1	16
4		37	9	10	1	8
5		26	5	4	1	9
6		16	3	4	3	3
7	1	12	3	2	—	4
8	1	8	1	1	5	1
9	1	8	—		5	
10	1	2	2		5	
11	—	1	—		3	
12	2	1	1		2	
13	3				2	
14	2				2	
15	2				1	
16	—				1	
17	2				4	
18	2				1	
19	2				1	
20	—				2	
21	—				—	
22	—				1	
23	—					
24	1					
25 or more	1					
Totals	21	165	28	42	42	80
Median	14	4-5	5	3-4	10-11	2-3

TABLE 3A

Private Universities
(21)

Positions	Number of Schools Reporting Positions	$30,000 and Above	$25,000 to $29,999	$20,000 to $24,999	$17,500 to $19,999	$15,000 to $17,499	$12,500 to $14,999	$10,000 to $12,499	$7,500 to $9,999	$5,000 to $7,499	Under $5,000
Advancement Program Manager	17	4	10	3							
Chief Fund Raising Officer	20		3	5	4	5	2	1			
Staff Member	20			2	3	6	5	3	1		
Staff Member	19				1	5	6	5	2		
Staff Member	16					2	8	2	4		
Staff Member	13					2	6	3	1	1	
Staff Member	8						3	3	1	1	
Staff Member	3						1	1	1		
Staff Member	3							2	1		
Staff Member	3							1	2		
Staff Member	3								3		
*											
Chief Public Relations Officer	19				7	4	6	1	1		
Staff Member	19				1	2	6	6	4		
Staff Member	17						5	3	8	1	
Staff Member	11						1	4	4	2	
Staff Member	8						1	2	3	1	1
Staff Member	3							2		1	
Staff Member	3							2		1	
Staff Member	2							1	1		

* (One institution has five more professionals at the $7,500 to $9,999 range and two more at the $5,000 to $7,499 range for fund raisers.)

TABLE 3A (Continued)

Positions	Number of Schools Reporting Positions	$30,000 and Above	$25,000 to $29,999	$20,000 to $24,999	$17,500 to $19,999	$15,000 to $17,499	$12,500 to $14,999	$10,000 to $12,499	$7,500 to $9,999	$5,000 to $7,499	Under $5,000
Chief Alumni Relations Officer	19			1		4	7	5	1		
Staff Member	19				1		1	7	10	1	
Staff Member	13						1	3	5	4	
Staff Member	4								2	2	
Staff Member	1									1	
Chief Publications Officer	14				2		5	5	2		
Staff Member	12						2	4	5	1	
Staff Member	8						1	3	3	1	
Staff Member	5						1		2	1	1
Staff Member	3								2		1

TABLE 3B
Private Coed Colleges (165)

Positions	Number of Schools Reporting Positions	$30,000 and Above	$25,000 to $29,999	$20,000 to $24,999	$17,500 to $19,999	$15,000 to $17,499	$12,500 to $14,999	$10,000 to $12,499	$7,500 to $9,999	$5,000 to $7,499	Under $5,000
Advancement											
Program Manager	94	2	1	16	16	24	20	15			
Chief Fund Raising											
Officer	93			5	6	24	14	27	16	1	
Staff Member	87				1	7	11	41	22	5	
Staff Member	37						3	17	15	2	
Staff Member	14							3	11		
Staff Member	2							2			
Staff Member	2							1	1		
Chief Public											
Relations Officer	143			1	4	7	19	41	64	7	
Staff Member	80					1		13	46	14	6
Staff Member	28						1	1	15	9	2
Staff Member	12								8	4	
Staff Member	4								3		1
Staff Member	1									1	
Staff Member	1									1	
Chief Alumni											
Relations Officer	135					3	10	44	59	15	4
Staff Member	25							4	12	8	1
Staff Member	3							1		2	
Chief Publications											
Officer	14							4	7	3	

TABLE 3C
Private Men's Colleges
(28)

Positions	Number of Schools Reporting Positions	$30,000 and Above	$25,000 to $29,999	$20,000 to $24,999	$17,500 to $19,999	$15,000 to $17,499	$12,500 to $14,999	$10,000 to $12,499	$7,500 to $9,999	$5,000 to $7,499	Under $5,000
Advancement Program Manager	20		1	5	1	6	4	3			
Chief Fund Raising Officer	16			1	1	4	1	5	3	1	
Staff Member	15					2	2	8	3		
Staff Member	6					1	1	2	2		
Staff Member	3						1	2			
Staff Member	3								3		
Chief Public Relations Officer	26				1	2	4	11	7	1	
Staff Member	16							3	11	2	
Staff Member	5								4	1	
Staff Member	2								1	1	
Chief Alumni Relations Officer	26						5	9	9	3	
Staff Member	6						1	1	1	3	
Chief Publications Officer	5							1	3	1	
Staff Member	1								3		
Staff Member	1								1	1	

TABLE 3D

Private Women's Colleges (42)

Positions	Number of Schools Reporting Positions	$30,000 and Above	$25,000 to $29,999	$20,000 to $24,999	$17,500 to $19,999	$15,000 to $17,499	$12,500 to $14,999	$10,000 to $12,499	$7,500 to $9,999	$5,000 to $7,499	Under $5,000
Advancement Program Manager	14			1	3	5	2	3			
Chief Fund Raising Officer	20				3	5	5	6	1		
Staff Member	12							3	6	2	
Staff Member	3							1	2		
Staff Member	2								1	1	
Chief Public Relations Officer	38					3	4	9	18	4	
Staff Member	13								4	6	
Staff Member	2									2	2
Chief Alumni Relations Officer	35							6	14	13	
Staff Member	8								3	5	
Staff Member	2								1	1	2
Chief Publications Officer	3							1	1	1	

TABLE 3E

State Universities (42)

Positions	Number of Schools Reporting Positions	$30,000 and Above	$25,000 to $29,999	$20,000 to $24,999	$17,500 to $19,999	$15,000 to $17,499	$12,500 to $14,999	$10,000 to $12,499	$7,500 to $9,999	$5,000 to $7,499	Under $5,000
Advancement Program Manager	21	1	3	10	6	1					
Chief Fund Raising											
Officer	28			6	3	7	8	4			
Staff Member	19					1	9	7	2		
Staff Member	12						2	6	4		
Staff Member	7						1	1	4	1	
Staff Member	3							1	1		1
Staff Member	1							1			
Chief Public Relations Officer	38		1	1	6	13	9	8	8		
Staff Member	40				1	5	10	16	15	5	
Staff Member	39					3	5	11	16	6	
Staff Member	33					3	3	5	17	7	
Staff Member	28						3	1	12	6	
Staff Member	21						2		3	5	
Staff Member	9								3	3	
Staff Member	7								3	1	1
Staff Member	4								2	1	1
Staff Member	3								2	1	1

TABLE 3E (Continued)

Positions	Number of Schools Reporting Positions	$30,000 and Above	$25,000 to $29,999	$20,000 to $24,999	$17,500 to $19,999	$15,000 to $17,499	$12,500 to $14,999	$10,000 to $12,499	$7,500 to $9,999	$5,000 to $7,499	Under $5,000
Chief Alumni											
Relations Officer	38			1	4	10	7	12	4		
Staff Member	29					3	2	11	10	3	
Staff Member	14						1	3	8	1	1
Staff Member	5						1	1	2		1
Staff Member	4						1		2	1	
Staff Member	2							1	1		
Chief Publications											
Officer	20				1	4	4	7	4		
Staff Member	16							5	11		
Staff Member	14							2	9	3	
Staff Member	8								7	1	
Staff Member	3								2	1	
Staff Member	2								1	1	

TABLE 3F
State Colleges
(80)

Positions	Number of Schools Reporting Positions	$30,000 and Above	$25,000 to $29,999	$20,000 to $24,999	$17,500 to $19,999	$15,000 to $17,499	$12,500 to $14,999	$10,000 to $12,499	$7,500 to $9,999	$5,000 to $7,499	Under $5,000
Advancement Program Manager	12			1	3	1	4	3			
Chief Fund Raising Officer	18		1	1		3	6	5	1	1	
Staff Member	4						2	1		1	
Staff Member	1								1		
Staff Member	1								1		
Chief Public Relations Officer	80				3	16	18	27	12	4	
Staff Member	34						4	8	17	4	1
Staff Member	20							3	13	4	
Staff Member	9								4	5	
Staff Member	4								2	2	
Chief Alumni Relations Officer	36				3		3	11	12	4	3
Staff Member	2							1	1		
Chief Publications Officer	14					1	4	6	2	1	
Staff Member	2							1	1		

TABLE 4A

Salary Increases of Chief Officers of Various Advancement Program Activities

Private Universities

(21)

Salary	Advancement Program Manager		Chief Fund Raising Officer		Chief Public Relations Officer		Chief Alumni Officer		Chief Publications Officer	
	64-65	67-68	64-65	67-68	64-65	67-68	64-65	67-68	64-65	67-68
$30,000 and Above		4								
$25,000 to $29,999	6	10	2	3						
$20,000 to $24,999	6	3	4	5				1		
$17,500 to $19,999	2		2	4	2	7		1		2
$15,000 to $17,499			2	5	6	4	3	4	1	
$12,500 to $14,999			6	2	5	6	7	7	4	5
$10,000 to $12,499			2	1	5	1	4	5	5	5
$7,500 to $9,999					1	1	4	1	4	2
$5,000 to $7,499										
Under $5,000										
Not Given	1						1			
Total w/Chiefs	15	17	18	20	19	19	19	19	14	14
Total w/o Chiefs	6	4	3	1	2	2	2	2	7	7
TOTALS	21	21	21	21	21	21	21	21	21	21

TABLE 4B

Salary Increases of Chief Officers of Various Advancement Program Activities*

Private Coed Colleges

(165)

Salary	Advancement Program Manager		Chief Fund Raising Officer		Chief Public Relations Officer		Chief Alumni Officer		Chief Publications Officer	
	64-65	67-68	64-65	67-68	64-65	67-68	64-65	67-68	64-65	67-68
$30,000 and Above		2								
$25,000 to $29,999	1	1								
$20,000 to $24,999	6	16			5		1			
$17,500 to $19,999	6	16	6	6	2	4				
$15,000 to $17,499	15	24	10	24	3	7		3		
$12,500 to $14,999	24	20	18	14	5	19	5	10		
$10,000 to $12,499	21	15	25	27	31	41	22	44	1	4
$7,500 to $9,999	7			16		64		59		7
$5,000 to $7,499			28	1	96	7	86	15	6	3
Under $5,000				1		2	9	4		
Not Given	1			2		2		1		
Total w/Chiefs	81	94	90	93	141	143	123	135	7	14
Total w/o Chiefs	84	71	75	72	24	22	42	30	158	151
TOTALS	165	165	165	165	165	165	165	165	165	165

* The salary study was made with two questionnaires, each sent at a different time. The first questionnaire had only one salary bracket in the $5,000 to $9,999 range, while the second divided the bracket in half, $5,000 to $7,499 and $7,500 to $9,999. Therefore, figures for the 1964-65 year are placed halfway between the two brackets because it is not known how many persons actually fell into each of the two brackets—(applies to tables 4B, 4C, 4D, 4E, & 4F).

TABLE 4C

Salary Increases of Chief Officers of Various Advancement Program Activities

Private Men's Colleges

(28)

Salary	Advancement Program Manager		Chief Fund Raising Officer		Chief Public Relations Officer		Chief Alumni Officer		Chief Publications Officer	
	64-65	67-68	64-65	67-68	64-65	67-68	64-65	67-68	64-65	67-68
$30,000 and Above										
$25,000 to $29,999		1								
$20,000 to $24,999	2	5	2	1						
$17,500 to $19,999		1		1	1	1				
$15,000 to $17,499	4	6	1	4	1	2	1			
$12,500 to $14,999	5	4	3	1	1	4	1	5		
$10,000 to $12,499	3	3	5	5	7	11	6	9		1
$7,500 to $9,999				3		7		9		3
$5,000 to $7,499			6	1	14	1	17	3	3	1
Under $5,000										
Not Given										
Total w/Chiefs	14	20	17	16	24	26	25	26	3	5
Total w/o Chiefs	14	8	11	12	4	2	3	2	25	23
TOTALS	28	28	28	28	28	28	28	28	28	28

TABLE 4D

Salary Increases of Chief Officers of Various Advancement Program Activities

Private Women's Colleges

(42)

Salary	Advancement Program Manager		Chief Fund Raising Officer		Chief Public Relations Officer		Chief Alumni Officer		Chief Publications Officer	
	64-65	67-68	64-65	67-68	64-65	67-68	64-65	67-68	64-65	67-68
$30,000 and Above										
$25,000 to $29,999										
$20,000 to $24,999		1								
$17,500 to $19,999		3		3						
$15,000 to $17,499	1	5	5	5	1	3				
$12,500 to $14,999	3	2	5	5	1	4				
$10,000 to $12,499	4	3	5	6	7	10	2	6		1
$7,500 to $9,999	2				1	18		14		1
$5,000 to $7,499			3		25	4	28	13		1
Under $5,000							2	2		
Not Given	1				1		2			
Total w/Chiefs	11	14	18	20	35	39	34	35	0	3
Total w/o Chiefs	31	28	24	22	7	3	8	7	42	39
TOTALS	42	42	42	42	42	42	42	42	42	42

TABLE 4E

Salary Increases of Chief Officers of Various Advancement Program Activities

State Universities

(42)

Salary	Advancement Program Manager		Chief Fund Raising Officer		Chief Public Relations Officer		Chief Alumni Officer		Chief Publications Officer	
	64-65	67-68	64-65	67-68	64-65	67-68	64-65	67-68	64-65	67-68
$30,000 and Above		1								
$25,000 to $29,999	1	3			1					
$20,000 to $24,999	3	10	1	6	2	1	1	1		
$17,500 to $19,999	8	6	1	3	1	6		4		1
$15,000 to $17,499	4	1	6	7	3	13	2	10	1	4
$12,500 to $14,999	2		4	8	13	9	14	7	3	4
$10,000 to $12,499			7	4	12	8	11	12	6	7
$7,500 to $9,999								4		4
$5,000 to $7,499			6		5		9		9	
Under $5,000							1			
Not Given			2			1	1		1	
Total w/Chiefs	18	21	27	28	37	38	39	38	20	20
Total w/o Chiefs	24	21	15	14	5	4	3	4	22	22
TOTALS	42	42	42	42	42	42	42	42	42	42

TABLE 4F

Salary Increases of Chief Officers of Various Advancement Program Activities

State Colleges

(80)

Salary	Advancement Program Manager		Chief Fund Raising Officer		Chief Public Relations Officer		Chief Alumni Officer		Chief Publications Officer	
	64-65	67-68	64-65	67-68	64-65	67-68	64-65	67-68	64-65	67-68
$30,000 and Above										
$25,000 to $29,999				1						
$20,000 to $24,999	1	1		1						
$17,500 to $19,999	1	3				3	1	3	1	
$15,000 to $17,499		1	2	3	5	16	1			1
$12,500 to $14,999	5	4	2	6	7	18	2	3		4
$10,000 to $12,499	3	3	3	5	24	27	5	11	3	6
$7,500 to $9,999			5	1	38	12	17	12	6	2
$5,000 to $7,499				1		4		4		1
Under $5,000						1	6	3		
Not Given				2		3	2	1		
Total w/Chiefs	10	12	14	18	78	80	34	36	10	14
Total w/o Chiefs	70	68	66	62	2		46	44	70	66
TOTALS	80	80	80	80	80	80	80	80	80	80